GUILT
FREE

Also by Thomas C. Oden

GUILT FREE

Thomas C. Oden

87-1703

ABINGDON
Nashville

GUILT FREE

Library of Congress Cataloging in Publication Data

ODEN, THOMAS C.
  Guilt Free
    1. Guilt. I.Title.
      BJ1471.5.O33   233'.4   80-15744

ISBN 0-687-16350-1

Biblical quotations, unless otherwise noted, are from The
New English Bible, © the Delegates of the Oxford
University Press and the Syndics of the Cambridge
University Press, 1961, 1970. Scripture references fol-
lowed by an asterisk (*) are from the King James Version;
those followed by a dagger (†) are from the Revised
Standard Version of the Bible, copyright 1946, 1952, ©
1971, 1973 by the Division of Christian Education of the
National Council of the Churches of Christ in the U.S.A.;
those noted Phillips are from the New Testament in
Modern English, copyright © J.B. Phillips, 1958, 1959,
1960, 1972.

MANUFACTURED BY THE PARTHENON PRESS AT
NASHVILLE, TENNESSEE, UNITED STATES OF AMERICA

*For my daughter
Laura*

Contents

Preface

The Laughter
of Unmerited Grace

There is a quiet laughter that pervades the biblical picture of guilt and freedom. It is the laughter of unmerited grace.

There is a glint of humor, a playful sense of lightness, an echo of unseriousness that drifts toward irreverence in the curious Judeo-Christian idea that God himself struggles against our sin. This is why we can approach the subject of guilt with nondefensive joy, as if we already knew a kind of "open secret" about it. You do not grasp that secret without the hint of a smile. Our own dreadful feelings of guilt are put in less tragic, more modest, perspective once the secret is out.

There are dozens of stodgy theories about what guilt is and how it works. All of them can be sorted into two piles: the "pass the buck" view and the "sin" explanation.

The "pass the buck" view always sees guilt as someone else's problem. No one ever admits responsibility. Guilt is said to be caused by subtle influences from parents and parent substitutes or social ills or genes or economic systems or *McGuffey's Readers* or bad movies or peer pressures. This is sometimes called the naturalistic view of guilt since it sees guilt as strictly determined by natural causes (nothing is ever willed); but no one will mistake its identity if we call the theory simply "buck-passing." Psychological sickness is thought to be the result of moral inhibitions and repressed energies. Health, therefore, requires overthrowing these oppressive moral constraints so that one can breathe free as a single, self-standing individual.

The alternative view is the "sin" explanation which says that guilt is the result of real offenses against real moral values that result in a disruption of the balance of moral virtues, out of which the symptoms of illness in due time may appear. Instead of attempting to overthrow these internal moral voices, therapies based on the sin explanation deal with them attentively so as to reduce our misdeeds, make up for harmful actions we have taken, and reunite us with a pacified conscience. For finally it is only actual misdeeds that result in real guilt, which eventually may work its way into psychosomatic symptoms. Frankly, I think the sin explanation is more in accord with the facts, even though it is prone to certain distortions.

Obviously the two diagnoses are opposites and the therapeutic goals are at direct cross-purposes. Modern politics, education, judicial administration, economic theory, and psychotherapy have bought into the pass-the-buck premise. Although the Bible is far more than a sad lament over sin, it is the basic sourcebook for the view that sin causes guilt.

The sin explanation maintains that the pass the buck theory is an expression of sin. The buck-passing view maintains that the sin explanation is caused by harmful overly protective parenting that needs to be therapeutically corrected.

I admit that my inclination, the natural preference I feel, is toward the buck-passing view. For I would prefer that whatever I have done wrong be seen as someone else's fault. But that very inclination is the strongest argument I know for at least some truth in the sin explanation. For passing the buck must stop somewhere, as everyone knows. Finally we come face to face with the fact that someone willed something. Eventually, the buck-passing explanation logically requires an agent, unless one is willing to live with the intellectual embarrassment of an infinite regress of buck-passers.

The title *Guilt Free* is a condensed code phrase that embraces several layers of meaning, all of which are axioms of biblical psychology:

★ Cheap, painless views of freedom from guilt can wreck havoc upon a heedless society.

★ Christianity's guilt-free Word differs radically from modern counterparts that tend to dodge the rigorous claims of conscience.

★ Christian freedom is not a denial of law, justice, or responsibility to the neighbor, but a celebrative ethical response to unmerited grace.

★ Far from being a sickness, the capacity for

constructive guilt is a normal and necessary correlate of human freedom.

★ The costly word of atonement—God's reconciling love made known in Christ who died for our sins—perennially remains the solid foundation for Christian celebration of freedom from guilt.

To penetrate the intricate layers of meaning in this compact phrase is the task of *Guilt Free*.

The thesis of this book is that there is no easy way out of guilt, as some buck-passing politics and therapies imagine. There is only one way to be free from guilt and that is to undergo the moral education of guilt, to listen to what guilt is trying to teach us about ourselves. As with many good lessons, the learning is not always easy.

Like a baby, this book has been easier to conceive than to deliver. It is a bit like a sculptor who has labored repeatedly to express a single striking vision, yet feels he never quite did justice to its beauty or symmetry. Those who have happened on my previous effort, *The Structure of Awareness*, published by Abingdon in 1969, (or before that my 1962 biblical meditation on *The Crisis of the World and the Word of God*) will recognize that those earlier studies sought to cover some of the same ground— to hammer out the same vision I want to work with here. I am not disavowing those previous attempts, but I now feel that some of their contours were awkward, some things were left unsaid, and above all our cultural history has changed so remarkably that the argument now needs to be shifted (especially to a harder line against easy promises of a bargain-basement way to freedom from guilt). To my mind these considerations have justified the decision to redo completely (almost to the point of unrecognizability) the first part of *The Structure of Awareness* as a separate book on the meshing of freedom and guilt in hopes that readers of the previous study will now find some questions answered more adequately here. In *Guilt Free* the earlier reasoning has been thoroughly recast into this new design, fitted particularly for springboard use by discussion groups, church schools, youth groups, growth groups, pastors, and general lay readers.

Three disclaimers are in order: (1) Since this book is addressed to laypersons, and intends especially to reach out for young readers without previous knowledge of either psychology or theology, it presents itself to them without an intimidating scholarly apparatus. So the footnotes and extensive documentation that were in the previous work (to which academic readers can still return) have been mercifully omitted here. Our purpose now is not to present the kind of elaborate evidence that might warm the hearts of strict empiricists, but rather (in the spirit of Irenaeus, Augustine, Calvin, and Kierkegaard) to speak simply and directly to the lay reader struggling to hear the word of scripture in relation to the experience of guilt.

(2) Readers who wish to see a fuller Christian interpretation of the psychotherapeutic treatment of guilt than we can give in these pages may refer to my previous discussions in *Kerygma and Counseling, Contemporary Theology and Psychotherapy, The Intensive Group Experience, After Therapy What? Game Free,* and *TAG: The Transactional Awareness Game.* I need not review those arguments in this short book. But

when readers come upon my tough-minded criticisms of psychotherapy in chapter 1, I would hope that they would not prematurely assume that my dissatisfactions with some aspects of psychotherapeutic practice come out of a lack of interest or engagement in the theory, methods, and practice of individual and group psychotherapy, but rather out of deep involvement with them.

(3) I trust that the hasty reader will not be tempted to an early dismissal of the initial argument as moralistic legalism without benefit of its concluding development and eventual reversal. A special corner in Critics' Hell is reserved for reviewers who leap to such a conclusion. Every author hopes that his effort will be read in full, not selectively. Any reader who selects just chapter 1 is likely to hear only the wretchedness of our problem described, missing the constructive definition of guilt in chapter 2 and the proper uses of guilt developed in chapter 3 which lead to an evangelical celebration of freedom from guilt by book's end.

Introduction

Beyond Narcissism

You know the feeling: You're reading a good book but come across a sentence that makes no sense. You blink, reread, thinking, "It's got to make some sense," but it doesn't. You stare numbly at the page, and finally skip it.

Later you go back. Someone has suggested that you missed the point completely. Ah! It makes piercing sense now. It even illuminates the remainder of the once-fuzzy argument.

The experience is like looking at a Gestalt diagram. At first you see the lower left as the front of the box. Only much later, after much strained

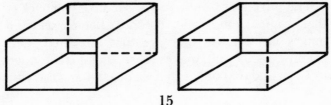

staring, peering, and discerning, do you "see" what others say they see so easily, that the upper right can also be the front.

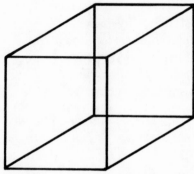

The pain of guilt feels something like our wrestling with the Gestalt diagram or the sentence that at first makes little sense. It is exasperating to not be able to "see" through its meaning. That ambiguous sentence is like the heaviness we feel when we do something cruel or cause some irreparable damage. Our conscience bothers us, attacks us from behind, meets us in dreams, makes us miserable. Why does conscience "punish" us? Did God "goof," as George Burns says in *Oh God,* when he created a sense of shame (like making the avocado pits too big)?

Guilt seems like an unclear sentence in an otherwise good story. Even upon closer examination it is reeling with perplexities and seeming contradictions. No wonder guilt has been the subject of the philosopher's interest for so many centuries. And it is not surprising that we have developed numerous "therapies" that propose to do away with it altogether.

The purpose of these pages is to take you back to that original enigmatic sentence. Let us see if it makes more sense than we first imagined. Our premise is that guilt makes sense, that it is intended by God, and that only when we hear what it is trying to say to us do we become psychologically healthy and free from its demoralizing side effects. There is a way to be guilt free, but only on the basis of listening intently to the message guilt seems determined to deliver. It is like a telegram delivery-person who patiently keeps ringing the doorbell, even when we are upstairs with the stereo woofing full blast.

GUILT FREE

Chapter 1

The Curse of Easy Street

Our theme—freedom from guilt—at first appears to be a harmless subject far removed from current events, political unrest, and cultural development. Yet on closer inspection, we find that we have on our hands a political hot potato.

Modern Chauvinism

By *modern chauvinism* I mean the smug assumption that all modern ideas are *superior* to premodern wisdoms. Older philosophies, psychologies, social traditions, and religious visions are, by that definition, "obviously" inferior to recent achievements (assuming that old = bad, new = better, newest = best). This opinion can be held by otherwise sophisticated people with tweed ties, Meerschaum pipes, and the aura of expertise.

I once had a university colleague who equated the nineteenth century (the era that discovered progress) with "dated and old-fashioned." The eighteenth century (the century that discovered toleration) in his mind meant "intolerant and prejudiced." The seventeenth century (the age of rationalism) meant "archaic and unreasonable." But for his most scornful epithet he reached as far back as he could into his vast historical repertoire of insults and said, "Medieval!" When he wanted to demolish one of his opponents, he would look down his nose and sniff: "Medieval," assuming that everyone else would naturally know that he was referring to "the most primitive form of dogmatic ignorance and misguided superstition." He became my living model of modern chauvinism. I learned quickly that many arguments could be clinched easily with anyone who assumed that new is a direct synonym for good.

Is this sort of chauvinism current among power elites? For all who doubt it, I like to challenge them to select any current issue of a major opinion-forming political or religious journal (such as *New Republic, Christianity and Crisis, Saturday Review*) and see how many examples per issue they can find of modern chauvinism—newer is better, older is inferior. If they find none on their own, I put myself to the test by agreeing to produce examples at the rate of one per minute, and usually make my quota.

Modern chauvinism assumes the absolute generic inferiority of premodern ideas. It discriminates *prima facie* against all older ideas, moralities, persons, and even words as blatantly inferior. All pre-twentieth–century individuals are stereotyped

21

as "outmoded" and treated as second-class citizens. Such thinking cripples our capacity to learn from historical experience. Above all it has hampered our ability to deal realistically with guilt. For modern chauvinism has nursed the illusion that we are developing ever-newer (=better) therapies and social strategies for diminishing the God-given sense of moral pain we feel in our inner selves when we fall short or do cruel things. Modern chauvinism has viewed guilt on the same level as the problem of the mosquito: something to be overcome by better methods of insecticide.

Meanwhile, we in recent religious leadership have spent a major portion of our time trying to find credentials acceptable to modern chauvinists. We have watched wave after wave of pop psychology and dubious social experimentation wash over the sandy beaches of modern Christianity. By now most of us have been washed over by so many of those waves of faddism that we are bleached, blistered, and waterlogged. This is evident by the fact that each new wave now has to "hype" its claims in rising decibels even to gain our faintest attention. Yet amid all this, many young people are discovering that premodern wisdoms may not be so tarnished or discredited as our modern chauvinist prejudices had assumed.

Our appetites are by now jaded by the ever-accelerating hedonic quest, by the frenetic hunger for consumption, for psychic or sexual highs, for hoarding chips and strokes, for packing sensory experiences into tight weekends. We despair of the pitiably little time we have to be finite persons (after all, only between birth and death). We hunger greedily for higher hedonic benefits at reduced interpersonal costs. Our heightened expectations about sexual fulfillment get pushed to extremity. It is into that context that drug experimentation has entered the scene, promising to transcend sexuality in creating the ultimate sensory experience.

As a society we are now bottoming out on this frenetic quest for sensate pleasure. It has been like riding a roller coaster—fun to get on, but you're sure glad when it's over. We are slowly beginning to learn that there is no three-day bargain vacation from the guilt we feel when we do wrong. I deal with young people every day. I see the depth of their hunger and despair as they one by one bottom out on this frantic search and begin to look for some deeper answer than the popular psychological panaceas available to them, (and "easy-out theologies" that, like violins, accompany these panaceas). It is a moment of reversal, the *metanoia,* of turning around.

My purpose is to give equal time to the classical Christian understanding of guilt and therapy for guilt. We will show that Christian scripture is more sound psychologically than its modern counterparts have assumed it to be, both in its transcending of the extreme individualism of Fritz Perls' prayer, Berne's polemic against the Parent, and Freud's stress on autonomy, and in its understanding of the overcoming of guilt through divine forgiveness (as distinguished from all our attempted humanistic self-extrications from guilt in prevailing social philosophies, psychiatric theories, and intensive group processes).

23

Here is the irony of our current social situation: It is the very youth who have been through sexual, psychological, and drug experimentation who are now disenchanted by the enchantments of secularization. Demoralized patients of psychotherapy are embarrassing the soft theories of guilt that have helped make the average time it takes for psychotherapy to be much longer than it needs to be. It is the children of modernity who are embarrassing the shaky assumptions of modernity. For our young people have been through moral experimentation without constraint, sexual experimentation without covenant, psychological experimentation without moral guidance, and drug experimentation without rational self-limits. It is the younger generation (better than the older) that are now dramatically grasping the fact that their *guilt did not go away* just because they had little or no parental restraint. We have learned to our astonishment that the capacity for guilt is a constitutive element of human freedom, a permanent fixture of human consciousness, which does not disappear even under the most permissive conditions. Even when we pretend that it is magically disappearing.

The problem of guilt is now being recognized as deeper than introjected parental influences, even though it is usually mediated through parentally taught values. It goes deeper than peer group pressure, even though the peer group may exercise a kind of parenting function. It is time to recognize that guilt has something to do with the way God is drawing us quietly toward the purpose of our existence.

Many young people are (painfully or insightfully)

24

going through this process of discovery today. These pages are addressed especially to them. They have been on the frontline of the battle to do away with guilt. They know firsthand the harsh consequences that occur when the parenting task is disavowed. They know what it means to "freak out" on moral acid, permissiveness, and vain illusions. They are now astutely grasping that conscience is more than custom, social etiquette, or blue laws. It is more than a first-grade schoolteacher's moral squeamishness. To understand that "more" is what this book is about.

Therapeutic Clones

Avant-garde social theory has tended to view every social problem as though it were directly analogous to the situation of an adolescent facing parental authority. True, adolescents must gain their own identity over against the more powerful parent world, break loose from external constraints, and "take charge of their own lives." But we have gained the curious impression from our modern chauvinist mentors that the adolescent struggle against parental oppression is the one and only standard pattern for all social change, all history, all human encounters. It is as if the Oedipal conflict of the son fighting against the power of the father to possess the mother were the only gene out of which all social conflicts have been cloned. This we learn directly from Freud (*Totem and Taboo, Civilization and Its Discontents,* and his 1931 essay on *Female Sexuality*), but we are just as likely to have learned it secondhand from the tribe of others who have followed in his train.

25

So it is that we have come to think of social policy as individual therapy writ large. It is becoming obvious that guilt-free therapy can be as disastrous for societies as it can be for individuals.

If the Oedipal analogy were absolute and all-embracing, then all social reformers would do exactly what troubled adolescents do—rebel against Big Daddy, the rules of the game, the associate dean, the establishment, in fact, any going "order." According to this analogy, anything "up there" with temporary power becomes identified in our minds as a "Pig Parent." Freud is not directly responsible for all the social analogies we have made, but they have arisen out of fifty years of the hegemony of his influence.

Much of the marvelous comedy of Steve Martin, Mel Brooks, and Woody Allen gets its energy from this adolescent struggle. The poorer comedies resort to showing us legions of sheriff's patrol cars diving into water, meringue pies pushed in the face of the mayor, banks exploding in slow motion, sheiks dancing with their pants on fire, etc., etc. Such comedy works because it sees the vulnerability of the establishment and laughs. I suspect, however, that the credibility of this comic premise is rapidly running its course. New forms of comedy are needed at this point in history that move out of an adult rather than an adolescent premise.

If we spend all our energies treating every social problem as a direct analogy to adolescence, we tend to lose sight of other (nonadolescent) developmental problems: the nurturing of trust (the problem of infancy), the development of basic skills (of childhood), and the hunger for integrity (the life-cycle crises of the older adult). The adolescent model indeed has some validity, not only for adolescents, but also for adults; but it does not build trust or help societies that face adult problems of social maintenance and intergenerational value transmission.

We are now at a very different place in our postmodern social history than the context assumed by the key advocates (Freud and Marx) of the adolescent analogy; for we are now mourning the loss of parenting. We miss our parents' historical experience. We have not assimilated their wisdom and social experience. We are on our own. Modern literature reveals that we have committed a kind of social patricide that has left us alone with our despairing individual freedom. The afterburn of this is the "bottoming out" process our young people are now undergoing.

Nothing seems more important to those who have bottomed out of adolescent politics and therapies than to rediscover *how to parent,* how to mediate values intergenerationally, how to build families and primary bonds. This requires relearning how to listen to the funded wisdoms of the past. It also requires learning again how to listen to our own conscience, how to follow the moral imperatives we all know very well, like "Thou shalt not bear false witness," "Love your neighbor as yourself," and "Do unto others as. . . . " Our problem is not that we do not know what these imperatives mean; we know all too well what they mean and have tried desperately to find some way to evade them.

Like a broken record we have repeatedly heard the charge that the traditional Christian view of guilt is *repressive.* This charge heads the list of standard charges against religion made by both Freudian psychoanalytic critics and Marxian social critics. But they view repression on very different wavelengths. Some theorists have combined these two (Marxian and Freudian) streams of criticism in a double dose (like two medications taken at the same time in which each increases the toxicity and risk of the other). Several of these theorists (Wilhelm Reich, Geza Roheim, Herbert Marcuse, Theodor Adorno, C. Wright Mills, Erich Fromm, Norman O. Brown) have exerted inordinate influence among educational, political, and therapeutic elites.

Their generalized charge of repressiveness needs now to be unpacked, taken seriously, and critically answered.

The Marxists say we are guilty of repression because our blessing is given to systemic injustice, and the Freudians point the finger of blame at us for repressing sexuality, the body, the libido, thus causing sickness. For both, atheism becomes the liberator. Their stance is in the tradition of the French Enlightenment (Voltaire, Rousseau, d'Holbach). If the cause of our ills is "God-blessed repression," the cure was to be atheistic criticism, revolution, and psychological analysis.

These criticisms by Freud and Marx were foundation stones for modernity. For what would modern consciousness be without either Freud or Marx? They are at the eye of the hurricane, the center of the century-old ideological storm (modernity) that has passed over and is now spending its fury and destruction.

The surest, hardest learning of postmodern youth is this: Much that has been called repressive

28

has only recently been recognized as a valuable, hard-won, beautiful fabric of social tradition, a precious gem of fragile human community, a finely balanced social process by which values could be passed on intergenerationally. We are now finding that our cultural achievements (wrongly dubbed repressive) are far harder to build up than they were to tear down. Meanwhile, neither the Freudian nor Marxian social systems have been notably successful in developing actual communities of the good life. Christianity is far from perfect in its historical communities and manifestations, but at least it *has* communities, while textbook Freudianism has no community, only the individual. Marxism indeed has community, but in most of its historical expressions it is more coercive and intolerant than most would wish.

Some of us have spent the last two or three decades under the tutelage of Freudian and Marxian theories struggling against what we thought was repression, only in mid-course to discover that we have inadvertently been destroying the very social fabric that makes both interpersonal intimacy and social justice possible. That sensitively woven mesh of social maintenance was carefully tended for centuries until we came along and found that it could be blasted to smithereens by our technical skills or eaten away by the acids of our "superior modern ideas."

Modern naturalism has "succeeded" in pummeling, mugging, and severely damaging venerable social traditions, intricately balanced moral systems, complex sexual mores, and bequeathed wisdoms that have been many patient generations of

29

grandmothers and granddaughters in the making. We moderns are experts, you might say, in instant destruction. The Demolition Derby is one of our most telling modern inventions. Like crazed Robespierres, we go about looking for something *else* to destroy, and find it very difficult to find anything. Modern chauvinists have gleefully enjoyed watching these baroque achievements and wisdoms crumble under the sway of vast, powerful, idiot-hearted technologies.

It seems almost too late to make the discovery that our young people are now having to make for us in the wake of the modern hurricane: *that the standard opponents of repression are far more repressive than the religious and moral systems they have opposed.* When we examine the actual social products, political, practical, and domestic consequences of the Freudian and Marxian programs we begin to recognize the depth of the new repressions and barbarianisms that have swept over us with a vengeance. I will give only two examples, but you can supply others from a wide range of experience.

As an example of disguised repressiveness by the antirepression critics, we have witnessed to our horror the recent history of Cambodia, a textbook case of theoretical Marxist messianism. The leaders of the Pol Pot regime came straight from the pockets of disillusioned French Communist intellectuals in the bistros of the Left Bank in Paris. These expatriate Cambodian students imported stilted "revolutionary" ideas into a vulnerable Cambodia, faint from international conflict, broken alliances, and economic dislocation. They simplemindedly applied the ideal theories they had learned from

30

their Marxist mentors in their purest form. They proceeded, textbook style, to eliminate bourgeois opposition, just as Marx and Lenin had demanded. The textbook said eliminate the profit system and its accomplices, so they promptly did away with the monetary system, the schools, the hospitals, the cities (!), and virtually the economy—all of this in the interest of a political dogma against repression! The social result: sadly it can only be called genocide. Marxist messianism displays a sweeping carelessness about human life in the name of an ideology of caring. The bluff of social revolutionaries who call Judaism and Christianity repressive itself needs to be called, for they have created systems of repression to match the most repressive regimes with which Jews and Christians have ever (wrongly) colluded.

As a second, everyday example of repressiveness done by the ideological opponents of repression, I choose an instance from personal experience. I have a friend who has been under psychoanalytic therapy for three and one-half years, who has spent about one-fourth of his income (approximately $14,000) on that care, yet after all that seems farther away than ever from solving his anxieties (which I consider embedded in the predicament of human freedom, and in some sense irresolvable). The dependency relation with his psychiatrist is now locked in; the client needs security and reassurance, the therapist needs clients, and the relation goes on.

As I listen carefully to him, what interests me is what he is being *taught* through the transference relation with his psychoanalyst: health is self-expression, especially sexual. This means an unrelenting campaign by his therapist to *repress the inner*

31

voices of his religious training, parents, and previous moral education, in order to move him away from "hangups" with "antiquated sexual taboos." His trajectory of sexual experimentation now includes three extramarital sexual liaisons, a short-lived homosexual episode, and a kinky venture into pornographic voyeurism that has left him all the more deeply mired in guilt feelings which his therapist reassures him have no basis in reality.

When his marriage threatened to break up, the therapist had no theoretical or moral defense for marriage and no reason to try to sustain the covenant; so the ship of his marriage was virtually *aimed at* the rocky shores, instead of trying to avert them. All of this has laid huge hidden costs on his two children for whom he has learned to disavow any significant parenting responsibility.

This has occurred through the covert moral instruction of a "reputable" psychoanalyst, licensed by the state of Pennsylvania to heal dysfunctional symptoms and improve psychological health! The therapeutic imperative has been: "Feel your own feelings; break free from oppressive moralism (parents, "conscience," superego), and gain ego strength—*but* I will not give you moral advice."

You may say that my friend got bad psycho-analysis, and I agree. But is it typical? The outcome studies of the effectiveness of psychotherapy are not reassuring. For the rate of cure of average psychotherapy is roughly equal to the spontaneous remission rate (i.e., the rate of disappearance of symptoms due to the passage of time alone). Does the psychoanalytic opposition to parental influence and prior moral learning make the predicament of guilt deeper? If you answer yes, then it is time to ask why, and whether there may be alternatives. The purpose of this book is to present an alternative.

The Plot Thickens

Now, as we lick our wounds and count our losses, we are beginning to see more clearly: In trying to get rid of bad feelings (the painful effects of guilt) we have also thrown out hard-won social achievements. We have abruptly turned off the messages that guilt is urgently trying to broadcast. It is as if a map to buried treasure were casually tossed aside among stacks of yellowing newspapers to be thrown away.

We have watched a long parade of television interviews of psychotherapists expounding the fashionable wisdom that guilt is not based on anything real. They beg us not to feel guilty, as if feeling guilt were itself the sin, rather than sin being the basis of the feeling of guilt. You do not effectively do away with guilt by dismissing the reality of the transgressions that cause it.

Hedonic exponents have tried their best to forget or ignore conscience. The playground has been vast, ranging from amoral Machiavellian politics and computerized scenarios of doomsday to laissez faire abortion, methadone maintenance programs, and punk rock for eight-year-olds. But our favorite arena of experiment has been sexuality. To an extent unknown in previous human history, sexuality has been treated as an amoral plaything or toy, like a TV Ping Pong game only more so. And this is supposed to be a major achievement. Such ideas are sponsored by the same folks who brought us open marriage (now closed), the $100/hour psychiatric fee, and the shifting of the national debt to our children's children.

We have proceeded on the hazardous assumption that if we only express ourselves in our anger, assertiveness, sexual interest, and so on, our neurotic denials and blocks will be magically overcome, and we will therefore become healthy psychologically, and probably even move toward a more just society. Then we sat back in our recliners and watched the televised social consequences of this mentoring: the loss of personal intimacy, the break up of solemn covenants, the metastasizing cancer of narcissism, the disavowal of accountability. Next we took our dazed consciences to psychotherapists for mending, only to find them teaching us that guilt is unreal, not related to any moral failure or sin, and that the imagination of moral failure is itself the sin.

Allegedly the needed "therapy" is to *de-moralize*. Prior to the twentieth century demoralization was regarded as a sign of ill health. Now demoralization (in the sense of the destruction of moral tenacity) has become a form of medical practice that has for a while gained public confidence, the esteem of the academics, and social prestige with a high cash value. But in all this we have gained no freedom from guilt. Rather, we have increased our bondage to guilt.

Indelibly imprinted on my mind is the strained face of a fifteen-year-old girl in a television interview. Two abortions already, she was soon to have a third. Asked what she had against contraceptives, she shrugged with shocking simplicity:

"Sex just feels better without them," which meant that abortion had heedlessly and blatantly become a means of birth control.

That portion of the interview was shocking enough: to realize that human life, God's first and greatest gift, is being bartered off thoughtlessly for the momentary élan of sexual pleasure. But the sequel was even more shocking. An "eminent psychiatrist" was then brought in to talk to the teenager and the television audience about the guilt that emerges out of the consideration of abortion. He approved of her low guilt awareness as healthy and suggested that if she worried too much about the morality of her action, it would further complicate her life. I have never quite gotten over that five-minute interview, and what it implies for our society.

Instead of the Judeo-Christian view of guilt being discredited as predicted, we are now surprised to find that its modern detractors are being discredited. We have lived long enough to see some of the social fruits of accelerated buck-passing. The fruits are bitter indeed. Now we realize belatedly that we have overestimated the power of modern therapies and social strategies to deliver us from real guilt and underestimated their power to demoralize a vast civilization.

The reversal is slow, but its direction is clear. Fewer young people are voting with their feet for the philosophy of unrestrained self-expression. When they do, they sometimes discover tragically—as did the friends of the eleven young people trampled by the crazed crowd waiting to get into the *WHO* concert in Cincinnati in December, 1979—that

35

unrestrained self-expression is potentially explosive in its demonic fury.

The Data of Discontent

What data can we submit to show that society has not fared well under the assumption that guilt is unreal? Such data are all too close at hand. I live in a state where a crime is committed every 83 seconds, a larceny every 3 minutes, a burglary every 5 minutes, and an auto theft every 13 minutes, an atrocious assault every 36 minutes, and a robbery every 37 minutes, a rape every 5 hours and a murder every 22 hours. Fifty-five percent of those arrested are under the age of twenty-one. There was a 15.3 percent crime increase during the past year.

I am wondering how close is the correlation between (a) the prevailing influence of social theories that provide easy loopholes out of any charge of real guilt, and (b) the evidence of deterioration of social maintenance and social cohesion. The evidence of deterioration appears to be broadly based and subtly expresses itself in widely varied settings: the annual increases of teenage runaways, the disavowal of parental functions, the impact of drug abuse on the felony rate, the loss of credibility for normative morality, the juvenile shoplifting statistics (51 percent are under 18), and such subtle clues as the dramatic increases of loan defaults, bankruptcies, and theft of books from public libraries. These are seemingly unconnected arenas. The connections lie, we hypothesize, in the way we have rationalized our way out of any hint of potential guilt that might emerge out of moral responsibility.

Statistics do not penetrate the depth of the dilemma, but they do show the surface: They reveal annually increasing recidivism rates for convicted felons, increasing unwillingness of victims or onlookers to report crimes due to the possibility of retaliation, low percentages of rape convictions, and alarming suicide rates. New York City, with a population of eight million, has over a half-million assaults per year. An infant born in the city and living there for a lifetime has one chance in sixty-five of being murdered. Those risks are higher than combat risks in World War II. All the while the modern chauvinists keep on assuming that we are making some sort of "great leap forward."

The "me" generation has learned its assertiveness training, the art of intimidation, and "how to become my own best friend." By now every graffiti writer assumes the *right*, civil or divine, to draw crude graffiti and genitalia on any public train or toilet wall. In recent years, not only has graffiti been exalted as a right, but it has lately even been pronounced an *art*. (Surely the proper next step will be to make it a part of the required curriculum in college humanities courses with an endowed chair designated for its perpetuation. Of course the chair is likely to get a bit marked up with four-letter words!) Meanwhile, the "me" generation's excessive focus on purely individual self-actualization has caused staggering costs to families, children, and marriages. The number of persons living in one-person households rose 66 percent from 1970 to 1980. *These are all signs of the demoralization of a society that has tried to live out a guilt-free existence, yet without the religious resources that would make freedom from guilt morally plausible.*

37

There is every reason to conclude that social neurosis and psychological pathology have increased under the widespread influence of the assumption that guilt is unreal. But do these data, strictly speaking, prove that assertion? Not directly, but they at least give pause to the modern chauvinist assumption that we can continue uncritically along the same path. What would it take to establish a scientifically credible causal relation between the guilt-free ideologies and contemporary evidences of social deterioration? The present state of sociological science makes such causal relations virtually impossible to argue on the basis of strict scientific empiricism. Admitting that such a causal connection is beyond the range of "proof" in the hard sense, we will have to be content to state our argument more modestly as an hypothesis for further inquiry: Demeaning social consequences have followed at least chronologically, and we believe causally, from the recent prevailing ideologies of low-cost freedom from guilt.

The permissively parented younger generation is now slowly beginning to rebound from the bargain guilt-free ideologies. Easy Street was supposed to be in our neighborhood, but no one can find it. In contrast to the standard profiles of what youth are supposed to be doing, the emerging generation is hungering for family continuity, moral stability, disciplined freedom, and historic identity.

It is ironic, therefore, that those (myself included) who have been longest schooled by "easy-conscience" theories of law, therapy, and education may be least prepared to meet the postmodern situation of lawlessness, moral sickness, and educational demoralization. Those of us who have been most deeply shaped by the ideals of psychoanalysis, social radicalism, the American Civil Liberties Union, progressive educational theory, and Planned Parenthood; those of us who have assumed that there is no real guilt (only parental oppression), no normative morality (only relative values), and no willed social pathology (only regrettable social determinants) may be least prepared to understand the recent reversal in our postmodern historical development. The revulsion against lawlessness only seems to us a little fascist and very counter-revolutionary. Yet is was none other than Adolf Hitler who wrote, "I am liberating man from the degrading chimera known as conscience." Sobering, isn't it? If that is the sort of "liberation" we are to expect from some, we had best beware. "When hopes and dreams are loose in the streets," observes Eric Hoffer, "it is well for the timid to lock doors, shutter windows and lie low until the wrath has passed. For there is often a monstrous incongruity between the hopes, however noble and tender, and the action which follows them. It is as if ivyed maidens and garlanded youths were to herald the four horsemen of the apocalypse."

In his journal of *The Last Years*, Søren Kierkegaard developed this haunting theme:

A man falls into the water, another comes past: now it has always been the rule that the other does not have the courage to save the man. But before the discovery of duties towards oneself what happened was that the second man skulked off and confessed to himself that he was a coward. Now, on the contrary, he does not skulk off

39

at all, but he stalks off full of dignity. This is duty to oneself. Eating and drinking have always been regular habits, but after this discovery they mean something else: they are duty to oneself. To see that one scrapes some money together was always the rule, but now it is also something meritorious—it is duty to oneself. In brief, such [persons] of duty as we have today were never to be found before, their whole life consists of sheer fulfillment of duty. What a splendid discovery—duties to oneself! What the moral philosophers have hitherto sought in vain, a way of presenting duties that will persuade [others] to do them, has now been achieved, namely, by making a duty of what [persons] like doing and will do in any case. My proposal is that since duties to God have now gone out we should now abolish duties to our neighbor as well, and treat the whole of ethics under the rubric of duties to oneself.

A century later we can now proclaim that we have gone Kierkegaard one better. For it is only in the twentieth century that "ought" has become a widespread symbol for evil, that moral law has been treated as an enemy of reason, that a sense of obligation has become an evidence of sickness. We have learned from our high priests of secularization, the psychologists (and religious leadership has colluded disastrously with them by assenting to their presumed moral "credibility"), that our first and essential duty is to take care of ourselves, to assert our selves, to seek pleasure and avoid pain, as if that were an outstanding moral achievement!

Christianity knows that the despair into which guilt plunges us leads us to a better point from which we can hear the good news of God's forgiveness. Meanwhile, conscience blocks every escape path that would feed the illusion that we can flee from guilt without escaping from ourselves.

Only God's love in its own time opens the door to move beyond guilt through the pardon that enables us to love nonpossessively.

The rich social insight of Jewish and Christian historical experience is as much needed now as in the darkest night of Western civilization. Christian communities have been dealing with guilt, confession, penance, obligation, restitution, and consolation almost two millennia before modern psychotherapy came along to "improve" psychological health in one sweep by doing away with the premise that guilt is significantly correlated with actual misdeeds or transgressions.

Modern psychotherapies have been right to see that guilt can create illnesses, but wrong to think that guilt could be circumvented cleverly or undercut easily without moral reformation and honest acts of reparation. While we have been casting ought-language out of our modernly educated vocabularies, the ought has returned with a vengeance.

The Myth of the Myth of Guilt

Some readers may wonder why I would pick something so harmless as psychotherapy as a target for jest and joust. Aren't the therapists working as hard as anyone, maybe harder, with the dynamics of twisted guilt?

After focusing my main professional effort for twenty years on the dialogue between psychology and religion, I now reluctantly have to conclude that the theological voice in that dialogue must stiffen if the dialogue is to mean anything at all. I can no longer back away politely from a clash with

41

mainstream psychotherapy concerning its naive treatment of guilt. I am not attacking psychotherapy generally, but only on this one point: liberation from guilt by avoidance of conscience. Freud made no minor mistake when he pitted psychological health against morality, ego strength against superego, individual therapy against parenting. These are indeed issues in which Christianity has a stake.

A fair share of our social problems today are due in no small part to the absolute blind trust we have put in psychologists to solve the enigmas of guilt on a naturalistic basis without any realism about the fallenness of freedom. I am aware that there are some psychotherapists who do not fit my description. When I speak of psychotherapy, I am thinking of the mainstream of Freudian and post-Freudian psychotherapies that have promulgated, promoted, and traded on the reductionist explanation of guilt. I am convinced also that many non-Freudian therapists (including some Third Force humanistic psychologists) have bought heavily into the unfortunate assumption that guilt can be treated essentially as a symptom to be happily removed. I realize, however, that there are some psychotherapists such as Karl Menninger and O. Hobart Mowrer (a minority, I believe, but some might debate that) who reject the "pass the buck" explanation of guilt and are struggling to offer some meaningful alternative to the mainstream. I can only say to these minority colleagues, "May your tribe increase, and I implore you not to take offence when I target the mainstream tradition of psychotherapy not for general malfeasance, but particularly for its mismanagement of the problem of guilt."

In seven previous books I have celebrated many achievements of psychotherapy and how they correlate with Christian teaching. I now press one specific criticism of mainstream psychotherapy: guilt. On this point most therapies are not only inadequate but counterproductive. They have deepened the pathology. Yet religious leadership has baptized, blessed, and commercially endorsed these cheap advertisements of guilt-free liberation without atonement or cost. We are in much the same hole that the ancient church fathers found themselves in at the last of the General Ecumenical Councils (the Second Council of Nicea, 787); they struggled against religious leaders "in name only, not in fact," who having become "fickle" had "corrupted the vineyard, and gathered in their hands nothingness by failing to distinguish between holy and profane." Shall we remain tolerantly quiescent in the face of similar misjudgments and amnesia? The Second Ecumenical Council of Constantinople (553) pinpointed the answer: "He who when asked concerning the right faith, puts off his answer for a long while, does nothing else but deny the right faith."

Some may say that I am objecting not to psychoanalysis but merely a popular misconception of psychoanalysis. What worries me is that Freud himself said so many things to tend toward eliciting such a misconception. Freud thought that there was a direct causal relation between "nervous illness" and " 'civilized' sexual morality." "We must therefore view all factors which impair sexual life, suppress its activity, or distort its aims as being pathogenic." He regarded the factor of sexual repression "as the essential one in the causation of the neuroses proper." That Freud pitted health against morality is clear from his view that "all who wish to be more nobleminded" tend to "fall victims to neurosis." In his 1908 essay on " 'Civilized' Sexual Morality and Modern Nervous Illness," he wrote, "They would have been more healthy if it could have been possible for them to be less good."

Freud's attitude toward conscience is reflected in his famous quip from his *New Introductory Lectures* (1933): "As regards conscience God has done an uneven and careless piece of work." Conscience is usually described by Freud under the category of "obsessional self-reproach." The superego (or parental surrogates) "represents the claim of morality." "Our moral sense of guilt is the expression of the tension between the ego and the super-ego." According to Freudian theory, "the super-ego is the representative for us of every moral restriction" out of which comes the repression that results in neurosis. The superego is "the vehicle of tradition and of all the time-resisting judgments of value which have propagated themselves in this [repressive] manner from generation to generation." The Freudian dictum that "repression is the work of the super-ego" explains the essential therapeutic intention of psychoanalysis: "to strength the ego, to make it more independent of the super-ego." It is on this basis that we allege that Freud pits social morality against health.

In his essay on "Dostoevsky and Parricide," Freud offered his own "explanation" of "the mental origin of guilt and the need for expiation." "The boy wants to be in his father's place [but] . . . comes to understand that an attempt to remove his father as a rival would be punished by him with castration. So from fear of castration . . . he gives up his wish to possess his mother and get rid of his father. In so far as this wish remains in the unconscious it forms the basis of the sense of guilt."

Our charge that psychoanalysis views all human problems using the analogy of adolescent rebellion is readily documented by Freud but nowhere more dramatically than in *Totem and Taboo* (1913), where he argued that "the beginnings of religion, ethics, society, and art meet in the Oedipus complex." *All* the problems of social ethics prove soluble on the basis of this one single point: "the relation to the father." He concludes therefore that guilt is absurd and meaningless, since we have "let the sense of guilt for a deed survive for thousands of years, remaining effective absurdly for generations." This primal guilt is based upon nothing morally real or objective. "Only psychic realities and not actual ones are at the basis" of the "legacy of feelings" that result in the "sense of guilt." Our guilts and inhibitions "go back to a merely psychic reality" (*Totem and Taboo,* Part VII).

The Boomerang Effect

This opening skirmish has led us to the preliminary conclusion that we are witnessing a wholesale mishandling of guilt in our society. The psychologists have set the pace by viewing guilt merely as a matter of guilt *feelings*. But the trouble is far deeper. It also extends to widely varied spheres of influence where the guilt-free ideology has tended to become dominant: judicial administration, education, economics, political theory, and popular religious leadership. In all these areas we are now witnessing a reversal of previous excesses, a "boomerang effect."

Judges hearing criminal cases have often viewed guilt not as a real offense against society, but only as an ambiguous result of social and economic deprivation, determined by outward circumstances rather than any responsible acts of will. On this basis, they have left victims unprotected and have promptly pardoned offenders, allowing them to return to mug, plunder, and rape again. Ironically, these judges have dishonored the self-respect of our antisocial citizens by assuming they have no self-determining wills.

But we are already seeing a reversal. Judges like "turn 'em loose Bruce" Wright, the New York magistrate with a notorious record for releasing accused felons, are now on the defensive. Everyone knows that prison systems have become schools for advanced crime taught by hardened repeat offenders for whom efforts at rehabilitation have by and large failed. Those briefly incarcerated come out of prison trained to prey on victims ever more astutely. Civil libertarian vigilance, to which many of us have been committed, has discovered better how to protect the perpetrator than the citizen on the street. The society has rights too, not the criminal only. A few years ago we did not raise that question, because we assumed that society was guilty, that the criminal was merely the victim of the ills of an evil society. No one could be held guilty because no individual was guilty.

By now history has caught up with us and deprived us of these blissful visions. The syndrome of soft justice has been harder on the poor than anyone else. The boomerang has already hit us in the flak jacket. We are down as a society with six locks on every door both in ghetto and suburb. We are now in the process of beginning to reverse that trend. We are rediscovering the behavioral change validity of older notions of *poenitentia, restitutio,* and *purgatio* (penitence, restitution, cleansing). All our liberal theological sympathies go against the harder attitude toward guilt and sin that is realistically required today.

Meanwhile, in the school systems, many experimental educators have been optimistically viewing guilt as a simple problem of knowledge to be overcome through scientific investigation and rational suasion. Sexual immorality, for example, has been treated as a problem for sex education, but what does sex education usually amount to? Essentially a dull, physical flowchart of sexual mechanics. All moral injunctions are ruled out with an absolutist vengeance (and an inconsistency that renders suspect their fancy theories of moral relativism). Isn't it in a sex education class that one would least expect to hear any talk of transgression of moral law? Such talk, it is said, would be "inappropriate to the occasion and inconsistent with the assumptions of education." A telling admission.

Uncommonly generous teachers, meanwhile, have the odd habit of passing nonlearners on to the next grade, with the embarrassing result that numerous schools actually graduate students still unable to read. Yet when attempts are made to remedy this absurdity by competency testing, the purists of the guilt-free educational establishment resist this fiercely because of their Enlightenment notions of innate goodness.

We have been through George Leonard's *Education as Ecstacy,* and other fantasy versions of education as uninhibited self-expression, that deplore any normative moral input. We have scars to show that we have been through years of "value free" scientific education that have left us value-impoverished and the public schools demoralized. We have already been hit on our report cards by that boomerang. By now we are beginning to see the reversal of the momentum that seemed unassailable only a short time ago. The new impulses call first of all for personal safety and restoration of order in the schools, then for an emphasis on schooling as socialization, discipline as the basis of freedom, and on the rigorous testing of learning outcomes—all traditional ideas of education predating modern "reforms."

The same fantasy of guilt as unreal is seen in *economic* theories of public debt. The notion of indebtedness is very closely associated with the root word for guilt (guilt, gold, and the older word for money, *Geld,* all come from the same stem). Visionary economists have rationalized deficit spending as a necessary tool to insure political programs and the bureaucracies that live by them. Keynesian (government intervention) economics has consistently stressed the values of current consumption rather than long-range production, the happy economics of spend now, pay later. As usual, the poor have been hardest hit by the inflationary results. We have printed money by the carload as a political expedient, hoping this would temporarily salve our wounded economy (and incidentally—keep incumbents in power), but all this has merely made things worse.

Young people are belatedly learning that the seductive notion of spend now, pay later is antiyouth. It leaves younger generations unprotected from the avarice and spendthrift policies of older generations. It leaves Mayor Lindsay's grandchildren still paying Mayor Lindsay's debts.

Guilt-free economics looks upon debts as ephemeral (remember the close kinship of debt and guilt in the history of language). I am thinking of economists like A. P. Learner who have offered oft-quoted rationales for painless public indebtedness, especially the idea that in national debt "there is no external creditor—we owe it to ourselves"—and that "national debt is no subtraction from national wealth." (Even interest payments on the national debt are alleged to be "no subtraction from the national income." See if you can follow his reasoning: "This can be shown most clearly by pointing out how easy it is, by simply borrowing the money needed to make the interest payments, to convert the 'interest burden' into some additional national debt. The interest need therefore never be more onerous than the additional principal of the debt into which it can painlessly be transformed.") Such arguments for guilt-free public indebtedness remain favorites of politicians, even when repudiated by many economists. We have been hit in the pocketbook by that boomerang and are now down economically. We, the parent generation, are guilty of a certain kind of child abuse from the point of view of long-range economic morality.

49

What is important now is that we recognize the striking correlation between *the economic theory that says debt is imaginary, the Freudian theory that says moral transgression is imaginary, the school system that views educational failure as imaginary, and the easy justices who see muggings and rape as mere social deprivation without guilt.* All are pieces of the same theological puzzle.

In the political sphere, have we done any better? Some have assumed that there is no sin in politics that could not be cured by throwing money at it. Even in the case of Watergate, with a few notable exceptions, the perpetrators did not consider themselves objectively guilty of any real offense. Rather, they considered their acts merely as the Machiavellian assertion of self-interest that was to be expected of anyone, and particularly anyone in politics. Watergate was the logical political outcome of situation ethics and (a fiercely absolutized) moral relativism.

What has theology been doing all this time? Rather than offer its distinctive gifts of prophetic judgment, candor about sin, and gratitude for providence, theology on the whole has been busy trying to accommodate itself to the Freudians, the soft justices, the Easy-Street educators, the spend-now-pay-later economists, and the big-promise political idealists. Recent theology has colluded with the modern idea that guilt is not real, and that it has obvious political, economic, and psychological remedies. Theology, too, has reduced the problem of guilt to social mechanics, political tinkering, and psychological determinism, and thereby withheld its unique gift at a time when society needed it most. Theology has in fact intensified this false hope of a quick fix on guilt with its own antinomian (lawless)

50

version of the gospel: God's mercy without human social effort, pardon without requirement, grace without covenant accountability, God's unconditional love without any mention of justice.

The corrective voice that has been missing in this crucial moment of cultural reversal has been the wisdom of classical Judeo-Christian psychology concerning guilt for our misdeeds and forgiveness as God's good deed. Christians and Jews have not studied the scripture, the rabbinic tradition, and church fathers well enough to be able to tradition them meaningfully to our children. It is now time to listen afresh and let them breathe new life into us.

The main point of this opening salvo: Across the board in our society we have mishandled guilt by assuming that guilt is not real, that it is a curable psychological feeling resulting from ill-informed mores or customs with no transcendent reference. In the fifth century B.C. Socrates was plagued by the same sort of "Sophists" who thought morality was "mere custom," not based on any real moral claim beyond human needs, instincts, and impulses. As such, guilt is not to be dealt with either by confession or moral reformation, but by psychological adjustment and social management. Once again we have seen these strategies fail. We now have on our hands a vast society in deep crisis due to the widespread bungling of the problem of guilt.

To the younger generation, to whom these pages are especially addressed, it matters urgently how we understand the dynamics of guilt and how we deal with it therapeutically. The rest of this book looks for an answer that does not spring the hidden traps we have described.

Chapter 2

Constructive Guilt

Suppose the happiness of a given day were determined strictly by the bowl you chose for cereal each morning. *But* you did not know that.

Doesn't our moral sense tell us that would be unjust? Somehow, we know that happiness *ought* to be related to the exercise of freedom. If things were as they should be, when we do some good, we ought to feel better; when we do rotten things we feel rotten. Even when we cannot see how the mesh works, we seem to know deep down that there is some hidden correspondence between the good will and the happy life. Guilt is a part of the complex instructional system that is trying to teach us that correspondence.

Yet we do see the righteous suffer, the wicked prosper, and the rain falling upon the oil wells of the bad guys. So we know that the correspondence is not just a direct and obvious one, but a mystery that may take a lifetime even to begin to penetrate. Ah! More than a lifetime, replies classical Christianity: It takes a perspective that transcends this finite sphere altogether to make sense of the guilt we feel within it. Only from the end of history can the distortions and absurdities of history make sense. Christianity sees history from the end of history. Jesus Christ is one way of talking about that end.

Before prematurely blending into the easy rhythms of Christian language about forgiveness, we must first give scripture a chance to help us understand how guilt tries to work for us, even when we seem determined to obstruct it. To do this, we must examine how our idolatries (the false gods we adore) intensify our feelings of guilt.

The Inner Judge

Running a self is something like running a government. Your decision-making process is something like governmental decision-making, with its three familiar functions: legislative acts bring the law or political decision into being; executive enforcement applies the law to specific situations; judicial review assesses whether the law is properly administered according to the constitution of the body. Every government must exercise these functions. Every self does something very similar.

The *legislator* within me tries to envision what ought to be done, how my human *future* might better take shape. The imaginative legislator looks ahead toward reformulating the human situation, venturing toward possibilities for unrealized options more likely to bring human fulfillment into being. My *executive* task is focused upon the *now*, the existing context with its possibilities and limitations. The realistic executive tries to enact the good that is envisioned in a given legislation within the stubborn limits of the present. The task is to see that the envisioned good does not remain in the limbo of vague possibility, but that it becomes a reality embodied in time. Without an executive, even the most inventive legislature is like a factory without a distribution or sales operation, or like a gifted artist without paint and brush to execute the masterpiece envisioned. My *judicial* task has a retrospective direction; it focuses upon *already* actualized decisions of *past* actions now up before the bar of conscience. Having envisioned an action and having executed it in the face of other choices, conscience then reflects back in order to judge the actual performance of the deed. Picture the self like this:

Government has......................	JUDICIAL tasks	EXECUTIVE tasks	LEGISLATIVE tasks
Self must...........	judge the adequacy of its own past decisions in relation to conscience	implement plans it has envisioned within present limitations	explore future possibilities and select from many options those most promising
The time reference is.......	past	present	future

The checks and balances of government are similar to the way individual awareness moves through time. It is I who bring myself to the bar of conscience, set forth evidence against myself, and call upon myself to defend my actions, much like a courtroom drama. The case is argued internally. I

54

am my own prosecutor and defense attorney. I judge myself toughly, both my ideals and the finesse of my implementation of them situationally, even under conflicting claims. Both prosecuting and defending voices within me appeal to values that I have long claimed to be identified with my own well-being. I listen carefully to their accusations and defensive arguments. In dreams the crucial exchanges are symbolically rehearsed.

The judging voice within summons me, whether I like it or not (and often unexpectedly) to live up to my cherished values and relationships. It calls me to sustain the solemn covenants I have made. Even when I do not invite or like its verdict, I feel its authority intensely and acknowledge its immense importance, since it is in the most intimate sense *me* judging myself. It is impossible for me to be a self-respecting person without this continuing judicial review. How else could I move self-correctively toward the goals which I identify with my own basic welfare or the common good? Without it I am a moral cripple, for I am denying my self-critical capacity to redirect my actions toward the fuller expression of reasonable freedom.

I cannot turn conscience off or on at will, except at the price of deep, neurotic denials of intensely valued relationships. I may pretend not to care, but because these values are internalized (their voice having become my own), I cannot break free from them anymore than I can break free from myself. When I muff the values I identify with my own better self, I must live with the painful memory that I have "missed the mark" (*hamartia*-sin) of my deepest intention. This self-impoed moral discomfort intends to perform the therapeutic function of rechanneling me toward fulfillment of my value commitments. This is why guilt is good and necessary in its own limited time and place.

The more precious a value is to me, the sharper will be the moral pain. Its moral force may become so intense that it may for a season virtually immobilize the whole will. Everything else must decelerate until guilt is dealt with. If there are repeated self-deceptions, the judicial process may itself become sick and neurotic. I may examine again and again one particular blundering episode. My mind may become mutely fixated upon one single horrible event which so powerfully symbolizes my value bungling that everything else gets blotted out for a spell. On a different day, that same event may seem quite insignificant. But in the moment of intensified guilt, I return in memory to the scene of the crime and yearn for some higher moral resolution.

The judge in me usually has work to do. I commit myself to projects that do not serve my long-range well-being. I struggle fruitlessly for ideals that cannot reasonably be achieved. My capacity to conceptualize the ought works at a much quicker pace than my ability actually to embody the goods I conceive. Every pursued good implies a dozen unpursued goods. Every moment spent on the achievement of one goal is time lost toward reaching other potential goods.

I cannot be a chooser of good without being a denier of other goods. I cannot be a self-legislator without being an obstructor of potentially good alternative self-legislation. I have a friend who distinguished himself as a floor leader in a state House of Representatives. He conceded that his most difficult task was to find ways of tabling or blocking the floor of mediocre or partly good bills in order that the truly excellent legislation could be passed and wisely administered. Similarly, many fine legislative ideas will go down the drain in the process of creative obstruction in order that the legislating organism might move forward with what it thinks are the most achievable alternatives.

So it is with individual decision. I deny moderately valued relationships in order that the ones more valued may be pursued. Then I must live constantly with subtle forms of painful memory that I have failed to be what I might have been. Repeatedly I find myself denying high ideals I have earnestly embraced. As keenly as any judge who sits on the bench and threads his way through highly competitive arguments, I too experience the crunch of competing values and value losses even in my best choices.

In this sense every serious choice has a tragicomic dimension: For it is impossible to be a human being without choosing, and it is impossible to choose without value denials, and it is impossible to deny values without guilt. That is a very simple thought, but it forms the core definition of guilt: *an awareness of significant value loss for which I know myself to be responsible*. Guilt is the self-knowing of moral loss.

Time gives to human awareness its specific character: Responsible freedom does not merely *have* time but *is* itself a relation to time. Moral choice moves through the present always with a backward glance to the past. My decisions must bear the constant burden of remembered value denials. Guilt, then, is not merely a vague awareness that some general values are being wasted, but my specific awareness that *my own* values are being denied due to *my own* irresponsible decisions. I may also experience a secondary sense of guilt over someone else's bungling. There are times when others set the conditions, and I eventually have to make a bad choice. But the point at which guilt begins to pinch is where my own will is directly responsible.

Choice Demands Negation

From the day we are born, we are invited into an extensive moral learning process. Life calls us to make tough choices and to be responsible for them. It ushers us into the pursuit of competing values hoping we will learn to distinguish the enduring from the fleeting, the beautiful from the ugly, the good from the bad. Parents, professors, and peers all point us toward proposed ideals, goals, and values to be incorporated and interwoven into the growing self. Growing up in a particular culture is an extended learning process in which one weighs competing claims, computes relative values, and orders long-range priorities.

Some values I hold tend to compete with other values I hold in the endless new constellations that are formed. As life emerges with its delicate shades of complexity, the judging process becomes ever so subtle and refined. The self confronts intricately competitive clusters of values in each new situation, which are often understood internally only by the person experiencing them.

To simplify, let us suppose that at a particular moment an individual is confronted with two competing relatively good possibilities. The "crunch" in human decision may be understood essentially in this way: *To decide means to affirm one good option at the price of denying a competing good.* To decide is to elect one value, but always at the cost of not electing another. By its very nature, choice never occurs without the loss of some potential (but rejected) good. So in deciding for any particular value, we live constantly amid inevitable value denials for which each of us is to some degree responsible. The weighty memory of value loss is built into human decision-making. Compressed into a concise formula: *choice demands negation.*

The prophet Joel compared decision to a knifelike cutting action. Considering a decision is like sharpening a sickle for harvest. When the grain is ripe, you cut it. Once you have cut through the stalk, you cannot undo your action or return the stalk to its previous state. So it is with human deciding (Joel 3:13). Once we slash through a choice between two competing values, we no longer hold our options open in suspended judgment. The judgment is made. Either/or. I get married, or I do not. I take the job, or I do not. I live in California or Ohio, but not both at the same time.

Biblical psychology looks out on the human scene and beholds "multitudes, multitudes, in the Valley of Decision!" (Joel 3:14). Our decisions are made in the presence of God. Decision is not just a here-and-now hedonic calculation. It always exists

59

in an actual context. Ultimately, the larger context of that smaller context is universal history and the giver of history. The meaning of universal history is the subject of Jewish and Christian prophetic teaching.

No one is exempt from the required curriculum of conscience: "When Gentiles who do not possess the law carry out its precepts by the light of nature, then, although they have no law, they are their own law, for they display the effect of the law inscribed on their hearts. Their conscience is called as witness, and their own thoughts argue the case on either side, against them or even for them" (Rom. 2:14-16). So, the internal dialogue goes on. We assess the lift and drag of our past actions. The inspection is rigorous. We try to see if we measure up to the law "inscribed in our hearts." We argue within pro and con. Sometimes we feel acquitted, sometimes conflicted, sometimes judged.

These judgments occur in an arena that Paul calls "the secrets of human hearts." In this setting of deepest interiority, the meaning of Christ's ministry is anticipatively and partially revealed, though it must await the end of history to be fully revealed for all to see (Rom. 2:16). Conscience is the scene of divine judgment. It occurs now in our hearts, and it will occur fully at the end of time. There is a connection in Paul's mind between what the heart hiddenly declares now and what God's judgment will ultimately reveal at the end of history (Rom. 2:12-16; I Cor. 4:1-5).

Paul applies this test of conscience to specific moral decisions, for example, whether one should eat certain foods considered to be unclean. "Everything is pure in itself," Paul says, "but anything is bad for the person who by his eating causes another to fall" (Rom. 14:20). There is no harm in abstaining from eating meat or drinking wine, so long as one does so with a clear conscience. "Happy is the man who can make his decision with a clear conscience! But a man who has doubts is guilty if he eats, because his action does not arise from his conviction" (Rom. 14:22, 23). Whatever Paul says elsewhere about forgiveness does not slacken the heavy stress he places upon Christian freedom as continuing to listen to conscience.

God's good purpose in giving us both law and conscience is not only to bring us to an awareness of our sin (Rom. 3:20), but also on this basis to point us toward the announcement that we are freely acquitted by God's grace through the redemption that is in Jesus Christ (v. 24) in "a propitiation accomplished by the shedding of his blood, to be received and made effective in ourselves by faith" (v. 25, Phillips). "This was to show God's righteousness, because in his divine forbearance he had passed over former sins" (v. 25†).

Conscience is the part of you that tells you what you *ought* to have been and done. If we had no word for conscience we would soon have to invent one, even in a highly permissive society, since human existence as we know it cannot be lived without reference to some sort of shared understanding of what is importantly valued. These shared values become internalized through parenting, schooling, and befriending as one grows up in a given culture. Although the specifics of these values and norms may differ widely from street to street, family to family, society to society, era to era, no human life proceeds without such moral imperatives.

When G. H. Mead speaks of the internalized alter ego and Freud of the superego and Eric Berne of the Parent, they are referring to this process of becoming "acculturated" (receiving and internalizing definitions of values through social tradition, but chiefly through parenting). To grow up means to accumulate a fund of these defining voices inside us. In time they seem to become our own voice. The parental voice that repeatedly urges me to "tell the truth" may at one time have been my father's voice, but finally it becomes (through internalization) my own voice in such a way that I cannot distinguish easily between the various sources. The divine address through conscience is always heard from within the frame of reference of such stored values or ideas of good behavior which have become so deeply internalized that their voices have finally become my own voice. Conscience is not acculturation itself, though it speaks through acculturations. Conscience does not exist in some ephemeral world, but in history. Where else could it be known if it intends to address human decision? Just as God does not cease to be the Holy One when present in our midst, so conscience does not cease to be a transcendent claim even while making itself known in all-too-human consciousness. Since we live and breathe in history, not as abstract beings, the divine claim comes to us always through particular people, events, symbols, and memories, never without them. How could it be otherwise?

So what do I know when I know my conscience? Quite simply, myself, my moral self through whom God calls. I know what I value and how deeply I share in a valuing community. In many languages the root word that we translate as "conscience" literally means "a knowledge I have with myself." It is that which I know when I know myself morally, the depth dimension of ethical awareness which alone gives moral credibility and dignity to person-hood. To imagine a person without conscience is to think of something less than a complete person. It is possible, at least temporarily, for me to avoid listening to my conscience. But when I refuse to hear my conscience, then I am not recognizing the claims of my own deeper self, and in due time I will try again to get through my defenses.

The Performance

Like a stage-hand arranging furniture before the opening curtain, our value assumptions are always at work. Long before the instantaneous moments of decision, they are there, carefully setting the conditions for the dramatic events that are to occur. We do not step out on the stage without knowing our lines.

After the curtain falls, we assess our performance. To the extent that it was inadequate, guilt flags consciousness. Guilt is the memory of any past action inconsistent with conscience and moral self-under-standing. I experience guilt when I do something that is inconsistent with my picture of who I am.

Who am I? As a teacher I must carry the burden of remembering myself from time to time in unteacherly moments of withdrawal or impatience in which it seems clear to me that I am failing to realize my vocational dream. As a father I bear the

63

memory of unfatherly moments of pride and desperation that are inconsistent with my picture of myself as a father. As a friend I remember unfriendly occasions of anger or insincerity that remind me of my inconsistency with my own self-image as a friend. So guilt strikes right at the heart of who I am. It forces upon me the discomfort of comparing my concrete actions with my moral commitments. It makes me restless with the obvious gap between my goals and my deeds.

This gap is poignantly portrayed in Shakespeare's Lady Macbeth, whose circumstances have caught her in a wrenching conflict of values. She desperately desires to be the queen, to have power, because regrettably that is the only means by which she could view herself as a potentially valued, acceptable person. But the human life that she has to sacrifice to the god of her ambition is also valued by her—more than she knew at first. When confronted with the moment of decision, when one or the other value must go, so overwhelming is her passion for glory that she puts the weight of her persuasive personality behind the assassination of the king. Later, guilt intensifies. For the rest of the play we see her portrayed in her compulsive awareness of the murderous deed, symbolized in her fantasies by blood on her hands. In wretched self-loathing, she hallucinates this pitiable symbol of the guilt-creating event. She knows that "all the perfumes of Arabia will not sweeten this little hand." Once done, no deed can be undone, No manufacturers' recalls are possible on our past acts, no matter how badly we have produced them.

What one feels in real guilt is that one is *incon-*

sistent with oneself. The depth of that rift is the measure of the intensity of guilt. Each person's moral fingerprints are different. The nuances of guilt may differ as widely as persons' values are varied. A psychopath may murder a relative and feel only twinges of guilt, whereas a shy recluse may feel overwhelmed with guilt after dialing a wrong telephone number. But whatever the specific shape of the misdeed, guilt is essentially the awareness that what I have done is inconsistent with who I understand myself to *be.* My image of myself is challenged and assaulted by my own behavior.

Yet in every misdeed, as Plato argues in the *Gorgias,* we are attempting to choose some perceived good. Even in the worst imaginable crime, such as premeditated murder, some good is sought. In the murderer's choice to take another's life, he is attempting desperately to choose some other imagined or perceived value which to his skewed vision seems circumstantially better—perhaps an intolerable obstacle is thought to be removed, a consuming hunger for recognition seems to be fed, or a terrible wrong allegedly righted. Seen exclusively from that momentary internal standpoint, at the instant of his decision he is choosing some perceived value which to him is worth the terrible risk and cost of murder.

Magnified Guilt

Almost anything can prick the conscience so sharply as to be temporarily immobilizing: an overdue bill, an approaching police car, a collection plate, a cool glance from the boss—you name it;

anything can do it. The smallest event becomes magnified to an immense scale. The minor misdeed becomes extravagantly symbolic of endless, irreparable value negations.

Magnified guilt is our awareness that some minor, otherwise inconspicuous, misdeed is sweepingly symbolic of our inveterate neglect of cherished values. Trivial events may trigger in us a cosmic sense of our fallenness. Magnified guilt may come as a sudden dawning that, by George, I haven't done it! Or, I have done it! It has a sudden character because its symbolic impact hits the consciousness with instantaneous force, exploding in every direction seemingly to the ends of the cosmos.

I remember a forgotten appointment which I had solemnly promised to keep (Oh, good grief!); I peel a parking ticket off my windshield, my third one this year (Why did I do that!); again I am late mowing my grass (And I seem to hear my neighbor calling my place Safari Country!). In each case I am "hit" by the abrupt, staggering awareness that my behavior is badly inconsistent with my self-image. These events point beyond themselves to the gap I feel inside between what I should have done and what I actually did. I need no billboards to get the message across—only the ordinary, daily occurences which remind me of my typical behavior and how it misses my good intentions.

This is why despair over guilt is a persistent complication of chronic intensified guilt. The symbolic exaggeration of the minor deed into a major predicament is grounded in the vague, despairing awareness that things will probably always be this way. I will keep on breaking appointments, keep on trying to beat parking meters, and keep on allowing my grass to grow to embarrassing lengths.

Just how I come to magnify particular symbols is wholly unique to my own special value orientation. On Guilt Tuesdays the symbolizing process works overtime. It transforms the slightest flaw into a federal case. I happen to be a lousy fixer of things around the house. My wife's entire family has always been expert, I should say, world class do-it-your-selfers. Whenever anything falls into disrepair, I feel called (in subtle and humane ways) to the bar of judgment. The truth is, I am not infinitely fascinated by household repairs—I'm far too busy doing my own "more important" things. The result is that even the most minor maintenance tasks, delinquently undertaken, remind me of my stubborn neglect of responsible duties.

My chronic occupational disease as a teacher is not returning papers promptly. The reason I do not hand back the papers with gusto is that I do not like to make fine decisions and evaluations, which may involve the pain of saying no to persons for whom I care. Grading essays reminds me not only of the fact that my teaching is not always getting through to students, but also that I am not a self-confident decision-maker when it comes to fixing an academic judgment using standards that are often ambiguous. Furthermore! When I was a student, I highly esteemed those rare efficient professors who handed papers back promptly. When I decided to make teaching my profession, I made a conscious decision that I was going to get papers back on time, since that had meant so much to me. Well, here I am, fairly deep in the ruts of a teaching role that is already locally famous for this chronic form of irresponsibility. I receive a set of papers, set them on my desk, look at them for several days, hope they will go away, and only after much prodding from students do I face the music and give them their feedback and evaluations. A moment of magnified guilt comes over me the instant I hear a knock on my office door and someone asks if the papers are graded. At that instant it seems as though I stand before the whole of heaven and earth condemned of persistent negligence.

Human existence is literally an unending flow of value choices and consequent value negations. One can find seemingly tragic value losses at any point where decisions are being made. Responsible decision requires being awake to the proportional values at stake in any given moment, being free to affirm one and negate another, free to dare to make decisions, and live within the consequent value denials, aware of the imperfection of all human choices.

Guilt is painful because it is ourselves saying no to ourselves with deep inner seriousness. In excess it can cause deadening depression, withdrawal, and inner demoralization. With greater maturity we learn to protect ourselves from simultaneous unfulfillable requirements. In any given moment there is no reason to feel guilty about not doing more than that moment's reasonable requirement. For no reasonable requirement demands more of us than we are able to fulfill. Yet we tend to fancy ourselves constantly under multiple conflicting demands which, if we fulfilled them all, would require a month to do any single day's work. When sixteen different demands impinge upon the narrow, fleeting instant, it is hard enough to meet just one of them, but often we feel it necessary to bear the guilt for not meeting the other fifteen as well. I am not sixteen people, but only one person. I can say only one yes to the singular claim of this moment, so I may have to learn to say fifteen other implicit noes. This is where we get hooked on our own best ideals. While reality calls us to one yes and fifteen noes we instead try to enact three resentful yeses and cower away from our thirteen guilt-laden noes!

The trail of guilt becomes more difficult to track when our footsteps are blurred by the winds and wash of time. Eventually guilt is not directed toward a specific deed at all, but only generally toward "the past." Just as anxiety (as contrasted with fear) does not have an object, so guilt often is experienced as a vague sense of value loss, without being tied to any identifiable times or persons.

The uneasy memory gets entangled on its own best dreams. It starts working overtime. It searches out the most horrifying experiences, the deepest breaches of value, the most rending remembrances of value loss. Neurotic guilt scans the horizons of the past relentlessly seeking out the most deplorable, hideous, and culpable acts which are least consistent with one's self-image. This process is similar to the infinite passion of intensified anxiety for seeking the worst conceivable possibilities in order to alert the whole organism to potential danger.

The Idolatrous Intensification of Guilt

A *god* is a finite value elevated to centrality and imagined as a final source of meaning. A god is some ordinary, limited value which becomes necessary for one's self-validation. A *value* is anything in creation which is regarded as good, any idea, relation, object, or person in which I have a serious interest, from which I derive some pleasure or significance, or in relation to which I feel a sense of obligation. Idolatry is an overvaluating of a limited value in such a way that it is regarded as pivotal for one's entire self-definition.

In short, *a god is a center of value by which other values are judged to be valuable.* Anything can become a god. Any good in the created order is subject to potential idolatry. In fact, it must be good, or it is not even a candidate for adulation. If it promises no fulfillment, it has no power to tempt us to worship it or order our lives around it. If education were not a profound source of human enrichment, then it could not become a potential source of idolatry; but precisely because it is of great value to us, it can be idolatrized as a source of absolute meaning in life. If our nation were not a rich milieu for value enhancement, then it would not become a source of idolatry; but precisely because it is of great value, it tempts us to make an idol of it. If my relation to my daughter were not a source of affection and delight, it could not become a potential idolatry for me; but precisely because it has been of great value to me, it can enter into my imagination as an absolute value. I am tempted to adore her in a way we both know to be disproportional.

70

The difference between a value and a god is that a value is known to be a limited, creaturely good (subject to death and the erosion of time), whereas a god is regarded as a final and absolute source of good and is therefore worshiped, adored, and viewed as that without which one cannot receive life joyfully.

We take good things (the flag, the vacation, the grade average, the 280Z, the stock market, the sales chart, the gang, etc.) and view them as if they were enduring sources of absolute value. Insofar as I regard limited, contextual values as necessary for my self-fulfillment and yet fail to follow precisely those values, I feel under the increasing pressure of guilt. Each idolatry ups the ante of the values at stake and guilt becomes magnified.

When we elevate limited values to the level of ultimate givers of meaning, we reinforce the power of guilt. As our sense of guilt intensifies, it becomes destructive. Our term for this awareness is "demonic guilt." We borrow the image of the demonic from prescientific imagery because it dramatically expresses the picture of being a prisoner to alien powers, captive to mysterious forces seemingly outside our will but which insidiously work to control the will.

Guilt of this sort becomes a burden inasmuch as we have no choice but to carry it around with us in our daily awareness, in addition to the ordinary weight of our usual tasks. It is as intimate to us as our very memory of ourselves. It is as heavy as our current awareness of past value negations. We cannot flee this tension since it is rooted in our very selves. Only when we go deeply to sleep are we

71

in some sense freed from the burden, but even then we are strangely condemned to play out in fantasy our basic relationships of guilt and lost innocence.

This brings us to our next major step toward the constructive treatment of guilt: It turns on the concept of idolatry as described in the scriptures. It may seem that talk of gods and idols belongs to a dated prescientific world-view. However antiquated the notion of idolatry may seem to modern psychology, its essential meaning is surprisingly pertinent, and even necessary, to an adequate interpretation of guilt. Biblical psychology is an extended commentary on the psychological consequences of breaking the commandment to "have no other gods," or idols (Exod. 20:3).

The prophet Ezekiel faced the crisis of his life the day Nebuchadrezzar seized Jerusalem. Israel's "dearest thing" (its national identity) had to be taken away in order that it might learn proportional valuing. Ezekiel recounts: "I spoke to the people in the morning; and that very evening my wife died" (Ezek. 24:18). His life companion was taken away at the same time his national freedom was taken away. But was this grounds for despair? No more for Ezekiel than Job, who amid radical loss, declared: "The Lord gives and the Lord takes away; blessed be the name of the Lord" (Job 1:21). He trusted God in the context of his own loss of family, wealth, esteem of others, of all that the world values. Ezekiel and Job were giving expression to the central historical learning of Israel: idolatry invites vulnerability to excessive loss. The hard road of captivity is never intentionally preferred, but through it a more proportional sense of valuing may emerge.

When our heart's desire is taken away, Ezekiel predicted, we will at first feel a numbness and immobility. But "soon fugitives will come and tell [us] their news by word of mouth. At once [we] will recover the power of speech and speak with the fugitives; [we] will no longer be dumb" (Ezek. 24:26, 27). The muteness will then be transcended by social cohesion, faith, and hope. In captivity we will have a new opportunity to relearn through detachment and discipline that earthly securities are not ultimate. Such learnings are being required of postmodern youth.

We learn from tough street experience that our gods are vulnerable to the erosions of time. Life forces us to relinquish values we have regarded as absolute. Anyone whose face is weathered by time knows that all created goods are vulnerable like grass and flowers—alive today, withered tomorrow (Ps. 90:6). The nations we love may collapse. The family or friends we adore may reject us. The good health we have enjoyed may deteriorate. The wealth we amass is vulnerable to depression and dissipation. Life (which is to say God) is the teacher who occasionally, but in time unerringly, instructs us on the vulnerability of our gods. In the long run there is no other moral classroom available to us except this one—life in time.

Put differently, God the Creator, the giver of creaturely values, is a "jealous" God (Exod. 34:14). Of what is God jealous? Our gods! It is God who finally challenges our gods. Eventually they crumble and fade because of their own impotencies. All the goods of creation are finally to be received as what they are—limited, finite goods, not God. No matter

73

how highly I value my family, my culture, my economic position, my technological comforts, even my society's best political achievements, I find that everything in time has the character of being given and being taken away. If I pretend that any of these values are unlimited, I live under a dangerous illusion. It is under just such an illusion that idolatrous guilt proceeds toward its bewildering consequences. For the more we make an idolatry out of limited values, the more powerfully is guilt locked in and reinforced. We then must live not only with the vulnerability of our finite values but also with the inner division of increasing guilt. When relative values are taken with absolute seriousness, the demonic grip of guilt is intensified, and we find ourselves in human bondage.

Constructive Versus Destructive Guilt

Only now are we able to refine the pivotal distinction of this chapter between constructive and destructive guilt. This difference is linked with the sharp distinction the Bible makes between legitimate finite goods proportionally valued and the demonic intensification of guilt that results from idolatry.

Normal, or constructive, guilt is based on proportional valuing. It is the constant pressure you place upon yourself to improve. Although this pressure is sometimes unpleasant, you know very well that it is necessary, otherwise you would not take it so seriously. Without it your behavior would slowly sink into the mire of lowered moral performance. To be free you need to give yourself the stinging reminder that your value commitments

74

are still valuable even though you have rejected them to some degree. Conscience issues a piercing call to our better selves, even while ironically it is making us aware of our worse selves.

But at what point does the positive guilt-creating function of conscience tend to become destructive, twisted, and neurotic? Precisely to the extent that limited values are elevated to ultimacy, they increasingly exert a demonic, oppressive force upon consciousness. As idolatry is reinforced through repeated decisions, it tends to grow to compulsive proportions, gets out of hand, and even masks its own self-deception. Neurotic guilt may finally express itself in psychosomatic symptoms that block normal functioning and attack at subversive levels.

Guilt functions constructively when lost values are beheld in a spirit of proportionality; when they are judged according to their real value. Choosing among limited, finite, contextual values is something like the experienced shopper who learns the details of the market well enough to make highly selective, well-timed value choices, alert to cost-benefit ratios and secondary consequences.

But we are easily conned into pursuing simple absolutes. Moral idealism ceaselessly beckons us to heightened expectations, increased requirements, and intensified imperatives, yet without giving us the moral power to change our way of willing. Modern preaching and theology, somewhat confused about exactly what it is called to do, has easily become enamored with just such idealisms and moralisms. Consequently, the dull-witted have come to think of Christianity merely as the boring attempt to intensify high ideals, rather than the good news of God's love amid our broken idealisms.

Does biblical psychology, then, merely ask us to value good things a little less? Does the Bible seek a reduction of guilt by an overall deflation of the currency of moral ideals, so we can live more comfortably with an uneasy conscience? That would exaggerate a valid point. Although the Bible holds that no finite relationship is of infinite value, it does not embrace an extreme ascetic view that the source of happiness lies essentially in the reduction of desire. Some ascetic strategies try to diminish desire and reduce all valuing so as not to allow any loss to become an overwhelming disappointment. According to this view, the less one values created goods, the happier one is.

In contrast, life-affirming Christianity hopes that love, desire, and appreciation of limited values can be increased or decreased to the measure of their real proportional value. Jesus does not call for a stark reduction of all finite valuing merely as a preventive measure against disappointment. He calls for a love of good things with an awareness that they exist within the boundaries of birth and death, and are therefore under the judgment of the giver and source of all value (Matt. 6:19-21).

To the extent that we are trapped by the overvaluing, idealizing tendency, we are not free fully to celebrate the limited but real goods of creation. Idolatry by definition is not an accurate assessment of creaturely goods, but an overvaluing of them so as to miss the richness of their actual, limited values. If I worship my tennis trophies, my Mondrian, my family tree, my Kawasaki, or my bank account, then I do not really receive those

76

goods for what they actually are—limited, historical, and finite—goods which are vulnerable to being taken away by time and death. When I pretend that a value is something more than it is, ironically I value it less appropriately than it deserves. Biblical psychology invites us to relate ourselves absolutely to the absolute and relatively to the relative.

Biblical Psychology

Why should we turn, at this point in history, to a renewed study of biblical psychology? Hasn't modern psychology made such significant advances on the crude, primitive psychological insights of scripture that they deserve little modern attention?

It could be argued that since the Bible is the Word of God, God's personal address to each of us, on that ground alone it deserves our most serious attention. But the case can also be argued on the following grounds: Modern psychology has not realistically penetrated the dynamics of guilt. The Bible does. Modern psychology has cut itself off from the very insights that would help resolve the dilemmas guilt presents to us. The Bible offers these insights. Far from having transcended biblical psychology, modern psychology urgently stands in need of it.

Major sources for biblical psychology are the psalms, the prophets (especially Jeremiah and Isaiah), the wisdom literature (especially Proverbs, Ecclesiastes, and Job), and much of the New Testament (notably Jesus, Paul, John, and the Pastoral Epistles). Implicit psychological understandings, however, are latent in all scripture.

A major premise of biblical psychology is the

joyful awareness that God knows "the thoughts of
our hearts" (Job 21:27; Ps. 53:11, 139:23; I Cor.
3:20). The heart is the center of emotive energy. It is
"out of the heart" that evil thought proceeds,
according to Jesus (Matt. 15:19*). Yet the heart was
known to be "the most deceitful of all things" and
"desperately sick" (Jer. 17:9). Who can fathom its
depths? Who can understand the emotive life, the
heart? God alone, according to scripture. "I the
Lord search the heart, I try the reins" (Jer. 17:10*).
At its depth, biblical psychology focuses less on our
private self-examination than on God's examination
of us (see Ps. 139:23).

"Keep thy heart with diligence," says the Proverb,
"for out of [the heart] are the issues of life" (Prov.
4:23*). It is from this inner center of passion, feeling
flow, and motivation that outer action comes. Some
behavior modification strategies try to change
outward acts first, hoping that in time basic drives
and motivations will be shifted. The Bible counsels
us to keep the heart wisely and the outer self will
reflect wisdom, for the body only expresses the
heart's desire. Accordingly, the highest psychological education is to apply our hearts to wisdom (Prov.
2:2*). But what is wisdom?

"The legs of the lame are not equal," quips the
proverb, "so is a parable in the mouth of
fools"(26:7*). Wisdom means seeing things in their
proper proportion, sensing the accurate value of
things. The reason the fool does not understand the
parable, or scripture, is that he does not behold
things in true proportion, as if his legs were not the
same length and that caused him to see everything
at a tipsy angle.

Scripture does not count it an easy task to give another person credible psychological counsel, for that involves facing up to guilt and working through value negations. A judgmental attitude makes the neighbor defensive. Effective reproof begins with empathy and respect for the person (John 4:1-42). Biblical psychology urges us to be attentive when we are admonished or reproved (Prov. 15:5). Through such counsel we gain a deeper understanding of ourselves; like an ornament of fine gold, so is a wise reprover to a listening ear (Prov. 25:12).

Since the writers of scripture have such diverse insights about human passion, motivation, guilt, anxiety, and other psychological themes, and since they speak out of many different historical contexts, it is a bit awkward to talk of a "biblical psychology." Perhaps it would be better to speak in the plural of "biblical psychologies," since biblical perceptions and observations vary so widely.

While there is no single treatise or research report in scripture that would stand up to the usual criteria of empirical psychology, no perceptive observer can doubt that scripture is saturated with wisdom about the same themes that the modern psychologists are constantly examining. So in this discussion we are using the term "biblical psychology" generally to refer to all these materials, insights, and probes of psychological themes in scripture, taken together in their interface, differences, and interaction. Biblical psychology is a psychology informed by scripture, a study of human behavior illuminated by the story the Bible tells. It views human passions from the vantage point of God's compassionate self-disclosure in history.

79

Chapter 3

The Proper Uses of Guilt

Guilt is a highly interpersonal experience, not merely something that stays within us. It is often when we "look one another in the face" (II Kings 14:8*), that we experience most deeply our value denials. Without words, body language reveals our lapses of accountability. This is why the biblical psychologists implore us candidly to "speak face to face," that "our joy may be complete" (II John 1:12).

It is in beholding each other face to face that we are reminded of our contractual breaches and covenant bonds. It is only face to face that both guilt and forgiveness are unveiled. The psychologists of scripture were attentive to those penetrating moments when we are "not afraid of the face of man" (Deut. 1:17*), willing to behold what is really there in the eyes of our neighbor.

"Now we see only puzzling reflections in the

mirrors," says Paul, "but then [in the last days, when history will be fittingly concluded] we shall see face to face. My knowledge now is partial; then it will be whole, like God's knowledge of me" (I Cor. 13:12). The ultimate interpersonal disclosure, according to Paul, awaits us at the end of history. We will then know history's meaning as God knows us now: face to face.

Innocence and How We Lost It

What is innocence? It is Shirley Temple dancing with Bojangles or Fred Astaire just falling in love. Even though it is too late for most of us to make a serious try for it, we are fascinated by innocence when we see it, or something like it. We see glimpses of innocence in the child, the Romeos and Juliets, in tragic heroes whose flaws do not erase their essential goodness, and music of Mozart and the poetry of Wordsworth, the popular characters like Charlie Brown or Edith Bunker.

What is innocence? "Freedom from sin, guilt or moral wrong," according to its dictionary definition. Like Melville's Billy Budd, the innocent seem to have no acquaintance with evil. They are uncorrupted by deception or guilt. They are guileless, simple, unsuspecting.

It is not surprising that such persons (supposing they actually exist apart from fiction), are sometimes regarded as naive, dull-witted, or unrealistic. Naive because there is so much evil around one wonders how anyone could overlook it. Unrealistic because once human freedom meshes with the fateful chains

81

of human choice, there seems little chance for snow-white innocence.

The implication is that a state of innocence is lacking not only in the experience of choice (the exercise of freedom) but also in knowledge—knowledge of oneself and of the nature of things. Anyone who has exercised his or her freedom to any noticeable extent is usually lacking in innocence. Why? Because of the inevitable tendency of freedom to *fall* from goodness to evil, from its best possibilities to something less than its targeted best.

According to a long-held tradition, we know what human innocence is when we look at a newborn infant (Isa. 11:6; Ps. 127:3-5; Matt. 18:10, 19:14; I Cor. 13:11). (If you have been responsible for children lately, you may wonder!) At least in the infant we can behold the situation of human freedom prior to distorted values and skewed perceptions, before anxiety and guilt, before there is any awareness of how freedom can go astray.

Innocence and guilt are direct opposites, yet each concept requires the other. In Latin *noxius* (guilt) is the contrary of *innocens* (lacking guilt); in German *Schuld* (guilt) is the opposite of *Unschuld* (innocence), and so it goes.

Biblical psychology argues in this way: Guilt is an awareness of the loss of good things for which I am responsible. If this is so, we must posit innocence as a stage of development prior to this awareness. Otherwise guilt would be fated to our human condition rather than chosen. So guilt must be learned and chosen, not simply caused mechanically like one billiard ball bumping and moving another. *Innocens* in the sense of unawareness of freedom's

82

bungling is unlearned, native, spontaneous behavior like the newborn child's, whereas guilt only emerges in human consciousness after a lengthy and complex learning process of value internalization and choice. Nonguilt (*innocens*) is a given in and with the organism itself and is therefore the "original condition" of the organism (before the "fall" into guilt). Although this observation has been long expressed in the biblical idea of the person being created in the image of God (capable of mirroring the goodness of God), it has been long neglected by scientific, psychological observation (which has avoided moral terms such as guilt and innocence like the plague).

Into the embryonic situation of *innocens,* the intrusion of birth occurs. At birth, the organism's environment is radically altered. Prior to the cutting of the umbilical cord, there was no independent, self-determining past. Suddenly, with birth, the self begins to *have a past* and to exist in relation to its past. Some primitive forms of memory doubtless extend back into the prenatal situation, but with birth there begins the active, conscious, self-aware, independent personal history of the organism, which moves increasingly toward acculturation, memory, self-direction, responsibility, and (you guessed it) guilt.

One pivotal text upon which the biblical discussion of psychological health hinges is the saying of Jesus: "Unless you change your whole outlook and become like little children you will never enter the kingdom of Heaven" (Matt. 18:3, Phillips). The healthy newborn child is open to his or her experience, astonishingly so. There is no self-deception, self-hatred, no distortion in awareness as with intensified guilt. If the infant experiences some loss of value, you get the message loud and clear. The infant does not conceal any feelings from awareness, as later inveterate guilt will learn to hide and repress painful feelings from self and others.

Can we sort out the basic phases of the transition from this primitive, relatively innocent, open experiencing to the burden of developed guilt? How does the infant "fall" developmentally from innocence to guilt?

The healthy infant finds himself in the presence of persons who seem to affirm him radically and value him unconditionally. It is only on this basis that he learns to venture, to trust, to explore his environment. The newborn is free to move into the frightening environment of reality-testing on the basis of what he or she assumes to be a total, overarching verdict of pardon from significant others for all real or imagined inadequacies. If such an unconditional pardon is not there, or if it is not perceived as being there, the child may be unable to receive the world trustingly. If it is there, it is simply there to be received. It cannot even be easily cancelled out. Most new parents are amazingly accepting of the inconvenient and troublesome behaviors of their newborn offspring. If a six-year-old were to slobber, yell at 3:00 A.M., or wet his bed, he would be in real trouble. But not a new baby—it seems as though absolutely nothing he or she does is "wrong" or even could be! The temporary verdict of pardon appears unconditional.

Only after a prolonged period of living under this radical verdict of pardon does the growing infant learn to discriminate and internalize parental values. Later, as the processes of acculturation and parental value assimilation proceed, the child develops a sense of "ought" shaped by learned and traditioned values. It is on the basis of this developmental process that the conditions for guilt emerge. At a much later stage the child learns that the pain of feeling his value denials causes him to sense a deep split in himself. This may lead him to distort his awareness of guilt in order to preserve his idealized self-image. He then begins to cast out of direct awareness some events which earlier would have been acknowledged and received into awareness. The dynamics of guilt only then become troublesome, because the symbolization of experience is no longer consistent with experienced feelings. Eventually, elaborate defensive strategies may be erected to protect these symbolic distortions. Depth psychology shows the difficulties of retracking the tangled web of self-deception, evasion, and hardened defense.

Radical Acceptance: Human and Divine

Having described the "fall" of the organism from newborn *innocens* to emerging guilt, we now ask: How does one regain freedom beyond guilt without crippling burdens of self-deception? Upon what grounds might some deeper self-affirmation be achieved in spite of one's bungled freedom? How can one learn to embrace one's past if it is clearly unacceptable in terms of one's assumed norms and values?

It is only possible wholeheartedly to accept the past if it *is* actually acceptable! But who is to say what behaviors really are acceptable? An individual by himself, friends, social history, or cultural environment? It is here that a strictly scientific explanation of guilt tends to run its course, so we propose, from a Christian vantage point, that the past is really acceptable only if the source and ground of the past has made it acceptable.

There is no solution to the problem of guilt if the past as such is in fact unacceptable, if the past is the permanent residue of irretrievably lost values upon which our human well-being and moral self-esteem depend. There is no solution short of a divine verdict by which the past is redeemed and its bondage broken by some transhistorical power. Genuine self-acceptance is possible only with the awareness that the past is in fact acceptable. If God is known as forgiving, however, wouldn't it be better for our sakes if he made himself known as such in a way that did not invite our further irresponsibility, license, or lawlessness, but rather communicated to us an ultimate sense of pardon with profound constraints upon us to future responsible action? It might seem flippant here to say that this is just the direction toward which a thoroughgoing humanistic analysis of guilt incompletely points and yearns, and of which biblical psychology speaks.

How does it happen that persons who have been ensnared in neurotic guilt come to increased self-understanding and freedom? What makes for constructive behavioral change in the therapy of guilt?

The Greek *axios* refers to value, or that which has worth. *Therapei* is also a Greek word referring to a skillful, personally helpful service rendered to one in need. A value therapy (or *axiotherapy*) would be a therapeutic service rendered to the valuing self which brings to clear awareness the implicit value structure out of which guilt emerges so as to direct us toward fuller functioning. The person suffering with magnified guilt stands in need of just such a reassessment of the idolatrized values which intensify demonic guilt.

In good human friendship (of which effective psychotherapy is a surrogate), the individual finds himself in a situation in which his own intuitive valuing process is radically trusted by another person. He experiences the unconditional positive regard of another human being who remains fully in touch with his own feelings. The chances for healing destructive guilt are increased when someone enters empathetically into his frame of reference, supports his efforts to retrack his wretched distortions of awareness, receiving and clarifying them. Then he may increasingly experience the capacity to embrace his own current experiencing process. Effective psychotherapy frees the individual from the burden of demonic guilt, not by making him innocent, but by freeing him to accept his lack of innocence and to act within the ambiguities of his own personal history without crippling self-deceptions or exaggerated guilt.

In an empathetic relationship, interpersonal dialogue may at times proceed on the basis of a moral moratorium or as a sanctioned retreat with a kind of "higher court verdict" that in some ways is much like a good parent's temporary verdict of unconditional pardon. An open context is permitted in which repressed feelings and guilt-laden

87

memories are brought into an accepting awareness. Strictly speaking, the distortions themselves are not applauded, but the distorting person is accepted (even if temporarily and with hopes of change). According to widely varied practitioners (Freudian, Jungian, Gestalt, Rogerian), the therapeutic process would not function well at all if it did not nurture an empathic dialogue in which repressed and distorted experiences are permitted to be freshly received into awareness. Thus, in a sense, psychotherapy strives symbolically to regain the fallen innocence, to find its way back through the flaming swords of Eden to the primitive paradisiac situation of newborn innocence.

What a person learns while undergoing effective psychotherapy is not that another empathic person agrees with his value system, but that he is valued as a person even amid his past value negations. That learning does not happen merely as an abstract idea—it must happen in a living relationship in which one person actually mediates to another such unconditional positive regard that its impact comes through to a keen level of awareness. Clearly we are not speaking merely of an *idea* of acceptance, but of an eventful *relationship* in which I find myself radically accepted and understood amid my twisted self-awareness by one who trusts his own experiencing process and mine.

Hidden underneath this therapeutic acceptance is the implicit assumption that the source and end of being itself is accepting, that really is not just a void, nonrelating absurdity, but that reality itself is reaching out to affirm and support the healing process. In order to be effective, psychotherapy must in some way mediate that active acceptance rooted in reality itself. If it fails here, it does not reach its deepest intention. It is not finally the therapist who is the source of acceptance. He or she is only a mediator of an acceptance present and self-revealed in reality itself. The good therapist performs the representative ministry of making that accepting reality known and felt in specific interpersonal communications.

When this happens, there is no ultimate basis in being itself for destructive, idolatrous guilt. One might speculate, even on a humanistic basis, that the giver of time wishes us to embrace our past. If this is so, then to live as if we were necessarily enslaved to neurotic guilt feelings is to live under an absurd assumption which has lost touch with the center of being itself.

That is why any profound attempt to track the footsteps of guilt leads us directly to the religious hope for divine forgiveness. For it is precisely this *implicit* therapeutic assumption (that despite our sins reality *is* accepting) which is made *explicit* in the forgiving verdict of God in the Christ event. Christian worship celebrates, and Christian preaching announces, a radical once-for-all divine verdict of pardon which has been rendered upon the totality of history. The past is viewed, as it were, from the end of history. It is now not only possible but imperative to conceive of guilt in a new way. A new birth of memory is permitted and required.

The name that summarizes all this for Christians is: Jesus Christ. The teaching that arises from this person and event is called atonement—the at-one-ment—the reconciliation of God and the

89

sinner through the Son of God who dies for our sin, thereby taking the burden of our guilt upon himself.

Elapsed Time

Christian forgiveness, however, presupposes an attitude of candid realism about the past. To "pass" something is to go by it and leave it behind. "*The* past" points to all former times. "*My* past" is something quite different; it is that small part of the cosmic past in which I have directly participated—that slender arena of time in which I have shared my bit of freedom in the shaping of the destiny of the whole, for which I am in some sense directly accountable. My past is my elapsed time.

Suppose my past were at any time revisitable and eternally repairable. Decision would then be quite meaningless. For if I can always redo my past, I need not take any present decision seriously. We know that is not the way things are. We make decisions that we can never redo. If we could at any point change what we have decided, there would be no present accountability. Viktor Frankl has convincingly shown that if there were no death, human freedom would be emptied of significance because we could postpone any decision indefinitely. If the past could at any moment be redone, if any decision could forever be remade, if every human judgment were forever accessible to revision, then human freedom would be neither significant nor responsible. So if you value your freedom, you must begin by valuing it within the context of an irreversible flow of time, where past time really passes away. To get

90

into this truth, fantasize one of your past moments as a marble statue created for all time to come, an occurrence that can never be changed or subject to retouching. We may change our minds about the past, but the past itself is out of our reach. It can never currently exist again for us except through the twisted and ever-elongating access route of our ability to remember it.

While the future is open to possibility, the past is not. It is "filled up" already with events that have been decided upon and are impossible to remake, or even revisit except in memory. The only way in which we can "change the past" is to change our current interpretation of it. Indeed, what we confidently call "the past" is constantly undergoing revision through our review of it. But reinterpretation takes place only within the strict confines of the present, while the past itself remains forever irretrievable.

The problem is: while I do not know my future at all, I know my past all too well. Existence is a constant choosing process. Choice requires denial of good options. So the past I remember all too well is a past heavy-laden with lost values. Some are so good that they do not let me forget them easily or cheaply. That "knowledge I have with myself" is conscience, or the *scientia* (knowledge) I have with (*con*) myself.

Although memory may retain fragments of "what happened," there always remains an unnavigable and ever-broadening ocean between the past occurrence and present memory of it. Yet every known past event is by definition a remembered event. And every remembered event is constantly

91

being reconstrued in the light of present desires, prejudices, and hungers.

However fragile, memory remains our only avenue to this vast range of past experiencing. Artifacts, geological formations, and written documents serve as extensions of human memory to assist in the vastly expanded recollection of human history and prehistory. Yet the time-bound character of awareness leaves us with this humbling insight: All that *exists* in the strict sense is *now*. Whatever else may have come to pass can never again be presently experienced; it can only be remembered.

In biblical psychology it is God who allows and requires us to summon the past into present memory. God does not allow the past to stay past until it has taught us what it wishes to teach. It keeps on reentering our present. "That which hath been is now," says the Preacher in Ecclesiastes, "God requireth that which is past" (3:15*).

The biblical psychologists do not counsel us to repress any memory of our inadequacies. Rather, they look toward confession and candor in the divine-human dialogue:

> The memory of my distress and my wanderings
>   is wormwood and gall.
>   Remember, O remember,
> and stoop down to me.
> All this I take to heart
>   and therefore I will wait patiently;
> the Lord's true love is surely not spent,
>   nor has his compassion failed;
>   they are new every morning,
>   so great is his constancy. (Lam. 3:19-23)

While the memory of guilt is far from pleasant (like "wormwood and gall"), it has the curative intent of restoring us into an awareness of the constancy of God's love, new every morning. God's mercy is not spent even with our worst misdeeds.

A major therapeutic aim of scriptural psychology is to heal and expand the memory. Many psalms focus on recollection. Much New Testament preaching focuses on reminders (Titus 3:1) and recollections (Mark 14:72) of God's mercy and goodness. In the Eucharist we "do this in remembrance" of Christ (Luke 22:19 *mar. c*).

Two word-pictures recur in the biblical images of guilt. First, the feeling of guilt is like owing a huge and growing debt. The premium is due, the bills are piling up, and no resources can be mustered. The self *owes* its significance, its worth, to values that bestow meaning upon it. The judgments I make upon myself are conditional upon the deeds I do to bring my values into being. So limited goods become for me "conditions of worth," that is, the conditions by which I judge myself to be a worthwhile person. It is as if I make a contract in my value clearinghouse with a high value subject to idolatry: I will be loyal to you, *provided* you bestow upon my life beauty, significance, pleasure, or some other desired good. If it happens later that I must break the contract in pursuit of some other potential value, then I find myself "in debt," so to speak. I owe something to myself that remains unpaid, part of me asks another part of me to pay up.

Second, the experience of guilt is like a *fall*—the Greek word for guilt, *sphalma*, has the connotation of losing one's balance and tripping. A step is misjudged and the whole organism collapses. (The Hebrew–Christian tradition has spoken of the disastrous *fall* of humankind (Adam and Eve) from an original condition of innocence into vast irresponsibility and demoralization). Guilt is essentially the human awareness that we have slipped and tumbled down from our original possibilities. To the extent that one's self-image is pretentiously exaggerated, it is all the more vulnerable to the experience of stumbling and falling into an abysmal awareness of inadequacy. Biblical psychology correlates the height of pride with the depth of the fall. "Pride *goeth* before destruction, and the haughty spirit before a fall" (Prov. 16:18*).

Of Adam and Eve it is said that they "hid themselves from the presence of the Lord" (Gen. 3:8*). This phrase expresses a rich correlation in biblical psychology between guilt and the sense of separation. In our awareness of our broken covenants, it seems fitting that we remain at a distance from those with whom we share covenant commitments. There is an inner logic in the distance we feel from others when we fail solemnly shared value commitments. We avoid the presence and the gaze of those who know us best. Thus the last person the sinner wants to meet is the holy God who knows us better than any other. Isaiah stated the point flatly: "It is your iniquities that raise a barrier between you and your God" (Isa. 59:2). The problem is not that the Lord's "arm is too short," but rather that we have distanced ourselves from God.

It is in this connection that biblical psychology beholds the subtle kinship between *guilt and grief*. It is not accidental that in almost every grief situation there is some residue of guilt feelings. Both guilt and grief involve an intimate memory of the irretrievable loss of a valued friendship. When a loved person is removed by death from all further possibility of this-worldly encounter, one experiences an intense value loss at two levels: Not only is the other person gone, but there is no future opportunity to correct past wrongs. That is a part of the shock of death. Death is experienced as a definite closing of the question of the possibility of reconciling broken relationships in this life (Jer. 26:7-15; Luke 23:1-31).

Persons near death are sometimes reported to have experienced visions of a heavenly presence or eternal glory. I do not wish to rule out or discount such visions, but they correlate with a psychological insight. To come near death is to come near the moment of being relieved of the burden of freedom. Having to decide constantly between competing values is a potentially demanding situation which we know will come to an end at some point, and that by definition is death. It should not surprise us, therefore, that death is ironically perceived at times as a relief—perhaps as an unsurpassed vision of release.

In another sense, as long as we exist, we are God's burden. According to Jeremiah, if we are asked what the burden of the Lord is, "you shall answer, 'You are his burden' " (Jer. 23:33). The Holy Spirit grieves over the endless distortions that come out of our exercise of our freedom. Only by divine mercy and patience does God continue to allow us the freedom choose poorly, with the hope of improvement.

95

Timely Choice

Opportunities do not happen every day. This is what defines an opportunity: some good becomes possible in a time-limited setting, and then it passes by. An opportunity is a fit time or favorable juncture of circumstances (from *ob* + *port*, facing the port, or coming into harbor). Biblical psychology is deeply attentive to the seasonableness of things. The prophets thought that God was doing special things in special, unrepeatable times. When decisions are delayed, options are lost that are never again recoverable.

To everything there is a time and a purpose (Eccles. 3:1). The biblical psychologists want to nurture in us a discerning sense of the differences between various times. Green opportunities do not call for purple responses. There is a time to embrace and a time to refrain from embracing. Wisdom has to do with knowing the difference. There is a time to plant and a time for uprooting. The wise person knows the difference. Scripture is looking for a sense of discernment, a sense of proportion about holding and releasing values. The Bible does not counsel us to always do the same things in extremely different times. How dull that would make us. Rather, we are called to "discern" the difference between varied responses fit for various times. That is the reason for which we are given our remarkable human brains: to use them wisely to make these judgments (Eccles. 3).

The root word for happiness has to do with the "hap" or the special opportunity of an occasion. Something is "hap*less*" if it is not fitting or is devoid

96

of good opportunity. To *happe* something in Old Danish meant to chance upon or happen upon something. So he is happy who responds haply, or fittingly, to changing occasions.

It is no small task to follow the biblical imperative to "redeem the time," to make good use of unrepeatable moments. "Use the present opportunity to the full, . . . do not be fools, but try to understand what the will of the Lord is" (Eph. 5:15-17). Each moment offers us a gift, the reverse side of which is a challenge.

Yet time is given amid distortions that the Bible calls sin. Scripture calls us to responsive love and mercy to all of life. To "redeem the time" is to hear God's call, respond to the divine claim, and do what is required in that given moment. What I do with my time cumulatively is my history. What you do with your time is your history. There are no flashbacks or reruns. You will only get one shot at next Tuesday.

We are searching for a Christian way of understanding God's fleetest gift: time. When we distort our relation to time with excessive guilt and anxiety, God does not give up on us. Individually we continue to receive the unparalleled gift of time, even when we have been poor stewards. Even when our track record is slow, God keeps on investing in us. Even when our batting average is low, God keeps on coming to our games. Even with an embarrassing string of losing seasons, God doesn't quit yelling for us and at us.

What is guilt trying to teach us? To discern the special claims of a given time and apply good judgment to it. What the Bible calls "getting a heart of wisdom" involves learning to flow in time with your sensitivities, memories, and imagination, yet keep your feet on the ground in the process. The wise person is one who "knows in his heart the right time and method for action" (Eccles. 8:5).

Some have learned to say to God "my times *are* in thy hand" (Ps. 31:15*). To merely say to another person for ten minutes, "my time is in your hands," is an exceptional act of trust. But to say that to God for all our times is a radical act of trust. Said to God it includes all past and future times. Yet without a fundamental commitment of this sort, biblical psychology concludes that we are likely to continue living unhappily in time, with distorted levels of guilt and anxiety.

Jewish and Christian psychology does not mince words: "Be attentive" to what is happening (Ps. 130:2). "Take good heed to yourselves" (Deut. 4:15†). "Pay attention!"(Prov. 8:5†). The unattentive are lampooned: "Noses they have, but they smell not" (Ps. 115:6*).

Idolatrous guilt conceals its trail. The last thing we may want to see is ourselves. So the double-binds go to work. The blinders are strapped in place. The tricks we play on ourselves to reduce awareness become tracklessly complicated. The comic image of falling into a pit we ourselves are digging is familiar to the biblical psychologists (Eccles. 1:8; Prov. 26:27; Ps. 57:6). "He himself shall fall into the hole that he has made. His mischief shall recoil upon himself" (Ps. 7:16). A related image is self-pollution: we pollute ourselves with our idols (Ezek. 20:31). The Bible does not miss the comic edge of the recognition that we worship "the work of our own hands" (Isa. 2:8). The temporary pleasure that comes from deception is followed by a kicker: "Bread of deceit is sweet to a man [or woman]; but afterwards his [or her] mouth shall be filled with gravel" (Prov. 20:17*).

Jesus exposed self-deception and hypocrisy with powerful, direct language: Outwardly you are like "whited sepulchers," but inwardly "full of dead men's bones" (Matt. 23:27*). Hypocrisy is like a monument that looks spectacular on the outside, but has uncleanness and death inside. "Let love be without dissimulation" (Rom. 12:9*). The wisdom from above is without hypocrisy (James 3:17). The decalogue calls us "not to bear false witness" (Exod. 20). "Let no one deceive himself" (I Cor. 3:18†).

When guilt has been pushed into the distorted forms of repressed memory, it may return through the back door of neurotic symptoms. It sometimes comes back disguised as asthma, migraine headaches, peptic ulcers, and other psychosomatic illnesses. We "punish ourselves," so to speak, with physical pain. The unconsciously administered "punishment" tries to atone for guilt and reconcile us with the internalized values against which we have offended.

At times our offenses are so obvious to us that they "run before [us] into court" (I Tim. 5:24). On other occasions it takes more time for the memory of botched freedom to overtake our defenses and self-deceptions. According to biblical psychology, there is a specific internal timing to the memory of a particular misdeed. While some of us "run to meet the judge," others have to be hauled forcibly into court. The Bible is trying to teach us a sense of reasonable proportionality about these recollections, not letting our offenses run away with us as if unpardonable, yet becoming enough awake to them so as not to delay too long until they cumulatively overtake us. Early, undelayed regular confession is commended.

Inevitable, but Not Necessary

At this point our knottiest question requires unraveling: Is guilt from the outset inevitable? Is human freedom predetermined to fall? Are we therefore fated to guilt, as though God tripped Adam in his fall? The biblical psychologists develop a more subtle point: Guilt is inevitable, but not necessary. This distinction requires some unpacking.

Supposing idolatry intensifies guilt, do we have reason to believe that idolatry is universal and inevitable? The Bible does not view idolatry as fated or necessitated by the very structure of human creation. It could have been avoided. Consequently, *demonic guilt is never fated by the God-given human condition.* It is chosen. Despite powerful social and environmental influences, the individual remains in some definite measure responsible for his collusions in guilt-eliciting events. Humankind is not *by nature* consigned to idolatry. That could never be affirmed by Jews or Christians who celebrate God's creation as good (Gen. 1–2; Ps. 19).

The tendency of freedom to fall into idolatry, however, invariably leads us into temptations which make destructive guilt a persistent and universally experienced consequence of human freedom. *So although human freedom is never from the outset strictly predetermined to fall into sin and guilt, it is forever tempted to succumb to the lure of idolatries; it then chooses modes of dependence which make idolatrous guilt the self-chosen bondage of all humankind.* Such idolatry is no longer a genuine expression of the highest human freedom, but rather a denial of it. Authentic freedom consists in living a nonidolatrous life of proportional valuing without inordinate pride, guilt, or idealization. So even if demonic guilt appears to be everywhere observable in the human scene, it is only a regrettable witness to the self-alienating character of human freedom.

One can only be guilty over that for which one is first responsible. There is no guilt without responsibility. But when we say (generically) "man is responsible," do we mean by "man" merely an isolated individual or a social process? Just as "man" cannot be viewed realistically as an abstract individual, so responsibility cannot be fully understood individualistically, as if a single person were abstractly accountable apart from the concrete claims of the social context. Not only individuals, but nations, families, and political systems in this sense experience guilt. Guilt can be a *corporate* as well as an *individual* experience. Neither side of the coin can be traded by itself. For each individual participates in a social environment that is always already distorted by guilt to which he or she contributes further. Upon careful observation we finally come to behold the awesome universality of guilt in every nook and cranny of human history, yet always as an act of someone's freedom in collusion with other wills. This is why the biblical view of universal guilt is not another "pass the buck" explanation.

101

"All have sinned and fall short of the glory of God" (Rom. 3:23†). There is no one that does not sin (II Chron. 6:36*). "If we say we have no sin, we deceive ourselves, and the truth is not in us" (I John 1:8*). We all "fall short," not simply because we are finite or limited in reason and imagination, but also because we willfully transgress the known good, tending endlessly to assert our private interest inordinately. To anyone who might prematurely imagine that he is without sin, Jesus replies: "Let him cast the first stone" (John 8:7). That is where we all "walk away," because we know the vulnerabilities of our own glass houses. The tension between our original uprightness and our self-chosen fallenness is seen in Ecclesiastes 7:29*: "God made [us] upright, but [we] have sought out many inventions." God offers us freedom to use responsibly. We abuse it—a central axiom of biblical psychology.

During the crisis of Israel's captivity, some were lamenting: "Our fathers sinned and are no more, and we bear the burden of their guilt." It is due to their sins that we have become "like orphans," their "yoke is on our necks, . . . our skins are blackened" (Lam. 5:3-10). A different interpretation appears in Jeremiah. After this period of purging, captivity, and return, a time is coming when "it shall no longer be said, 'the fathers have eaten sour grapes and the children's teeth are set on edge'; for a man shall die for his own wrongdoing; the man who eats sour grapes shall have his own teeth set on edge" (Jer. 31:29-30). The Bible holds these two points in creative tension: we are aware of our deep corporate involvement in guilt such that the sin of Adam and of each of us affects all; and to that

102

corporate involvement each of us adds our own particular "twist" or version or tonality to the sin of the whole; yet God promises to renew his covenant with his whole people, as with each of us, to forgive our misdeeds, and restore us into covenant fellowship.

The Similarity of Opposites: Guilt and Anxiety

As I wandered quietly through the ancient Ras Shamra ruins some time ago, I was struggling mightily with my own guilt and anxiety. There, literally in the midst of the uncovered bones of history, as I walked through the gutted foundations over which the dramas of life had been played more than three thousand years ago, I realized: These people surely must have felt guilty and anxious just like me. As I picked up tiny broken shards of bowls that had once been put to daily use, it struck me that these people must have felt in the early Iron Age and before that the Stone Age much the same brokenness I was now experiencing. They too had struggled to feel reconciled with past misdeeds; they too worried about precarious futures. Guilt and anxiety must have felt to them much like my own feels to me.

Suppose another three thousand years went by. Suppose someone else were standing at that same spot with the same conditions of human freedom and responsibility. They too would be struggling to accept their past and enter their future. That put me in touch not only with my own feelings but with others who experience the same conditions of costly freedom that I do, who know what it means to live uneasily with a past and face an uncertain future.

Few live seriously without asking the question: How shall we deal with our "has beens" and our "not yets" without demoralizing guilt or immobilizing anxiety. Persons of all times have fought those same inner battles: guilt toward the past, anxiety toward the future, and boredom in the present. Biblical psychology has long been interested in understanding these vexations and positively redeeming them. God's good news offers a practical way of living out of the past without excess guilt, toward the future without undue worry, and in the present without deadly boredom.

It is a deceptively simple point that *human awareness exists in time*. Time inconspicuously sets the conditions for the many folded layers of human awareness. Although human awareness quite literally *exists* only in the present, it never exists without the push, pull, and drag of passing and emerging times.

Guilt, anxiety, and boredom are grounded in good motivations gone astray. The energy of guilt focuses on past misdeeds. The potentially creative concern of anxiety becomes excessively fixed on exaggerated visions of possible disaster. The syndrome of boredom becomes fixated on despair over a dull, ill-fated present, as if now were a lock with the key thrown away.

The more deeply we penetrate the anatomy of one of these "structures of awareness," the better we can grasp the dynamics of the others, because their hidden structures are similar. When guilt is compared point by point with the key elements of anxiety its mystique is exposed and demystified. The kernel of much biblical psychology could be reduced to this: as the human problem in relation to the *future* is an anxious attempt to control the uncontrollable, in relation to the *past* it is the futile attempt to rechoose what has been irreversibly chosen. We pretend to have power to decide the future in advance (which is as yet undecided), while we are forever trying to redo the past (which is done and not redoable). The comic side of our frustration is seen in the fact that we want heroically to *do the future and undo the past,* to give form to empty possibility and to reform what we have formed. Neither is possible. However anger or arrogance or infantile omnipotence may protest, the past remains forever formed, and the future remains as yet unformed.

Guilt and anxiety function symmetrically with the curious similarity of opposites. They work in opposite directions, one through memory, the other through imagination, to alert the self to past value losses or future threats to values considered necessary to its existence. The formula is: Whenever we symbolize the future as a threat to value, we experience anxiety. When we symbolize the past as a loss of value, we experience guilt.

But can we claim that these insights have any usefulness, or application, in dealing constructively with guilt? Their practical consequence is that guilt is now seen in its proper proportionality: *If your guilt is limited to your awareness of your past, it has no legitimate authority over your future. Similarly, your anxiety is limited by your relation to your future.* Anxiety has no legitimate power over your past. This observation can be tested by asking, How far is it possible to become directly anxious over a past occurrence? Admittedly one may become anxious over the future, potential, consequences of some past occurrence, but in that case the object of one's anxiety is only possibility, not actuality. For there is no way to anticipate the past.

Anxiety involves anticipation of a threatening possibility. The past cannot deliver any possibilities. Anxiety's limit is reached when future threats are exhausted. Similarly, one may *indirectly* feel guilt by *imagining* oneself responsible for a possible future value loss, but in that case again guilt is directed toward the *past*, toward the *remembered* image of oneself as a potential value loser. For no one can remember the future! The temporal boundaries of guilt are reached when the claims of the past are exhausted.

Chapter 4

Guilt Free

We approach the final turn of this journey: How does Christianity's guilt-free Word differ radically from its modern chauvinist counterparts?

Biblical psychology beholds the human emotions from the vantage point of their being beheld by God. Biblical psychology understands the human passions and feelings from the point of view of their being understood by the mercy and love of God. The reality of the past is finally clarified only in the light of God's address to it, God's costly atoning for it. Were it not for this, biblical psychology would hardly differ from other psychologies. Instead of exploring our jaded perceptions of our sorry past, biblical psychology dares boldly to ask how God redeems it.

Such a bold approach to psychology is vulnerable to perplexities and limitations. It cannot claim to be an easy substitute for empirical investigation, but it can complement and amend the assumptions of scientific approaches to behavior change. It can form the basis for deeper psychological intuitions and behavioral transformations than are possible on the basis of reductive naturalism, which locks freedom into causal chains and reduces guilt to social influences.

Speaking of Amazing Grace

We are at the point of a major transition. The stress now is upon God's action toward our guilt, not our frail attempts to atone for or cancel out our own guilt. The biblical psychologists focus on what God has done to change and restore the very situation that elicits guilt. At the Lord's table, both our weak-willed efforts at self-redemption and our weak-eyed analytical attempts to fathom the dynamics of guilt are engulfed by the mystery of grace.

Yet at this table we are constantly vulnerable to the charge, never easily answered, that our language about God actually does not refer to anything scientifically demonstrable and therefore does not finally mean anything. Why then should I persist in pursuing an inquiry into the human past as though it had been dealt with by God? Because I am persuaded that the truth of the human situation is adequately revealed only through such an effort. Only by reference to the self-disclosure of the giver of history is the meaning of history knowable and therefore the past really understandable. If human responsibility finally means responding to reality, we cannot endlessly neglect the question of the *divinely beheld reality of the past* in favor of the more tame question of how *we* behold our pasts. But how can we presume to speak or know about God? The rest of this book will make little sense unless we answer this question with greatest care.

We know nothing of God except as God makes himself known. Just as I can know little of you (except perhaps a few externally reportable facts) unless you decide to reveal yourself vulnerably to me, likewise we know nothing about God if he does not disclose himself to us in actual encounters and real historical events. If God is known as love, it is only because he has made himself known in loving deeds. If he is known as faithful in covenant, it is only because he has made himself knowable through actual covenant relationships. Christian teaching is wholly aboveboard in clarifying this pivotal presupposition out of which it speaks.

This is why the biblical psychologists cannot proceed without constant recollection of a series of crucial historical *events* through which our timely choices are illuminated. The Hebraic tradition remembers and celebrates the exodus event as the central salvation occurrence through which the merciful God makes himself known as Deliverer from bondage. Similarly, Christian worship remembers and celebrates the unparalleled events surrounding the life, ministry, death, and resurrection of Jesus as the crucial salvation occurrence through which God makes himself known as the One who atones for our sin. In these pivotal events of exodus and messianic fulfillment, the Jewish–Christian tradition has come to see the meaning of universal history mirrored. That mirroring is what

109

theology is about: the attempt self-consistently to clarify the meaning of universal history as it is illuminated by the mighty deeds of God, understood through faith.

Faith in Christ can only be properly understood from its own center, since it is a response to a personal encounter that is only meaningful in the full sense to those who respond to it. Faith exists not on its own initiative, but only as a response to something which has gone before it, namely, revelation. We do not penetrate deeply into the meaning of faith unless we come first to grips with the revelation to which faith witnesses. All this depends on a continuing community of remembrance. For if revelation occurs in history, then faith must be passed on through a witnessing and worshiping community, otherwise it would die out in one generation.

Although Christian faith celebrates God's self-disclosure in nature, and history generally, as well as inward life and interpersonal experience, it does not regard any of these as synonymous with revelation. For in neither nature, subjectivity, or portions of history is the will of God unambiguously disclosed. God is revealed only in the whole of history, and that implies the end of history. Christianity looks at history from its end. In Jesus, the people of the New Testament understood that they encountered the end of history.

The Christian community's authority for speaking of this ultimate revelation of God is fourfold: *scriptural* truth *experienced* in life, made intelligible and self-consistent through tough-minded *reasoning,* and mediated through the historic Christian *tradition.* All talk about God in the Christian community is called to be responsible to these criteria. No one of these criteria exists wholesomely without the corrective of the others. It is only through a *traditioning* community that faith hears and responds to the word of God. The writing and canonizing of *Scripture* is itself an act of traditioning by a living worshiping community. The witness of Scripture and tradition becomes intelligible, however, only when symbolized in terms that are *experientially* meaningful to oneself and others, and only when *reasoned* through with internal self-consistency.

We are proceeding straightforwardly with the assumption that God has made himself known. Who says so? Finally I must take responsibility for saying so, but I do so with the companionship of a whole community of persons spanning many cultural varieties of humankind and twenty centuries of history. Christian faith is not just a private judgment, although it certainly is a personal decision and commitment upon which one stakes one's fundamental self-understanding.

But could it all be based upon a hoax? It is conceivable that Christian faith could be a gigantic conspiracy or mockery. But this is just where each believer in the historic tradition has been willing to take a risk. Christian preaching announces the promises of God. Every hearer finally has to decide for her or himself whether these promises are true.

Do we then finally have no proof that God forgives? We must ask, proof in what sense? Our way of looking at the world is always molded by the community of discourse in which we live. Christian faith exists in such a community, just as the Marxist participates in a community that interprets history, the artist lives amid a community of aesthetic meanings, and the scientist lives out of a venerable scientific tradition. If you ask for proof, you ask for reliable evidence in relation to some reference group or tradition of discourse, some community of understanding. Since we grow up in different communities of discourse, we appeal to different criteria to establish the truth. Likewise, Christian teaching lives primarily out of a multi-cultural, transgenerational community of commonly shared meanings based upon Scripture, tradition, reason, and experience.

But could not all of these ideas about God merely be, as Ludwig Feuerbach said, a projection of our own needs? There is much truth in that. Many of our ideas about God *are* merely human wishes. But the Christian faith begins with the audacious assumption that God has in fact revealed *himself* precisely *against* our illusions about him! It is on God's own initiative that the Christian community has been called forth to witness, not merely to our human needs or preconceptions about God, but to God in his own eventful self-disclosure.

With this introductory clearing of the path, we are now ready to ask how Christianity's guilt-free promise differs radically from modern chauvinism's cheap version of the same. Our thesis is that the Christian's freedom from guilt is of a wholly different genre than the freedom from guilt proposed by hedonic self-redemption.

112

The Remedy

The logic of classical Christianity is disarming: If the hidden cause of magnified guilt is idolatry, then it follows that a remedy for idolatry would reverse the psychological momentum of magnified guilt. Idolatry is difficult to reverse, however, because it is always motivated by some good, or at least something that is absolutely perceived to be good. So to pursue any "remedy" for idolatry appears to the idolater as a "remedy for something good," which seems absurd. So the momentum of idolatry is not easily reversed. Nothing will stop it but trust in God. But how do we learn to trust in God? What school can we enroll in? Is trust possible? That is Job's question, also Jeremiah's and the Psalmists'. That is the enigma pondered by the Bible's keenest exponents of psychological insight.

Trust in God, instead of our gods, comes only when we grasp the trustworthiness of God. But where is that beheld or perceived? Where would one go to look at it or examine evidence of it? Short of God making himself credibly known in history as trustworthy, there is little hope that we could learn to trust God. Yet this is precisely what is understood to have happened in the history of Israel and the Christ event. In Jesus' resurrection above all something "clicks": God is trustable, even in death. We share in Jesus' death and resurrection by having faith similar to his in the same God who raised him from the dead. God convinces us of his trustworthiness by taking up our cause, taking our sins upon himself, sacrificing himself for our transgressions.

Idolatry loses its power as we learn to trust in God

113

beyond the gods (absolutized finite values) we have worshiped, which in turn have intensified our guilt. God educates us quietly, painstakingly, lovingly, in proportion to our ability to hear and learn, into a relation of trust, first by showing us the impotence of our gods, and then by encouraging us step by step to take increasing risks in trusting in God beyond our gods. In revealing himself as the One wholly worthy of our devotion, God also illumines the relativity of all relative values.

To the secular moralist, this relativization of finite values may sound as though God were the enemy of admirable human loyalties. There is some truth in that. God may have to struggle on our behalf against our fierce attachments to finite goods in order to wean us away from their false securities, so that we may finally learn to trust in the Eternal One who stands invulnerable to all the hazards of time and the "slings and arrows of outrageous fortune." But with patience the Holy Spirit teaches us to celebrate even our temporary value losses with the longer-range awareness that all created things are as grass, of relative value, subject to passing and death, yet point beyond themselves to the giver of all creaturely goods.

The essence of idolatry is a subtle transaction or collusion between my will and my most cherished value. I agree (tacitly, implicitly) to absolutize that relative good, provided that it will promise to render to me an ultimate benefit—to bestow meaning upon my life. But with faith in God that collusion is annulled and reversed. The empathic God teaches me that life is possible and even better without such complicating idolatries. So divine

114

empathy constitutes a counterassault upon the very premise and foundation of magnified guilt. Under the pedagogy of cross and resurrection, I learn that I do not need my guilt-intensifying gods anymore to make life meaningful. With the unconditional pardon of God, the self is liberated to *renegotiate its contracts* with all its gods that awesomely had been considered unnegotiable. One is free to shop the market of situational values and learn anew to buy, create, sell, and receive finite value possibilities in newly emerging contexts.

But we have not yet reached the most decisive phase of the reversal effected upon guilt by divine forgiveness. For it is through our idolatry that *we* ourselves had hoped to be valued. Through our idols we have yearned to find *ourselves* affirmable as persons. We had trusted these gods to deliver us into some plausible self-affirmation in which we ourselves would be actually accounted worthy and valuable.

Suppose, however, that you should find that you yourself are valued just as you are, not for the values you create or transmit, and thus without the "benefit" of your gods! Suppose you discovered that *you* are in fact positively regarded, even unconditionally loved, even in spite of the failure of your idolatrized goods to render their promised benefits! That would indeed be a remarkably liberating force against the bondage of idolatry. It would make your frantic quest for self-affirmation through idolatry quite absurd, outmoded by the radical character of the divine affirmation, and simply no longer desirable because of its vulnerabilities. That is precisely what the New Testament alleges to have occurred in the salvation event.

Atonement: A Canceled Debt

Do we then have on our hands a new past? What becomes of the past that God has "canceled out"? If it should be the case that God himself has acted so as to affirm the total cosmic past, then how is our past to be redefined? If it should be true that a divine verdict has in effect reconstituted the past or mercifully embraced it despite its distortions and value losses, then what might that conceivably mean for our own subjective experience of guilt?

The gospel in essence announces: *We are being unconditionally valued by the giver of values amid our value negations.* Through Christ's costly act of suffering, crucifixion, and death for our sins, we learn that we are being prized, judged, positively affirmed, received, and loved by the source and end of all finitude, even and precisely amidst our real guilt over our real sins.

Scripture does not merely teach the *idea* that we are being valued despite our value denials. It celebrates and proclaims a particular historical *event* in which we are once and for all unconditionally valued amid our value losses. Valued by whom? By the unconditioned source and end of all finite values. The concept of being unconditionally valued amid our value negations can only be grasped adequately on the basis of an actual relationship and *occurrence* in which we are concretely, unconditionally, and personally valued

116

amid our value negations. This saving event Christians call Jesus Christ.

From the limited viewpoint of our internal self-perception, we may continue to *feel* guilty before our own negated values and gods; but our condition before God, from the point of view of the ground and giver of values, has changed. We exist in an undiminished covenant with the unconditional valuer. How one temporarily *feels* about oneself is different from who one *is* before God. The truly penitent are forgiven, despite the tenacity of all remaining guilt feelings to deny that amazing grace.

So how does guilt-free Christianity differ from its secular counterparts? It frees us from demonic, self-destructive guilt through atonement: God's Son dies for our sins. We are freed from guilt-laden idolatry by being shown that the One who gives both creaturehood and finitude, and finally the One who takes it all away in death, has made himself known as trustworthy. If I am unconditionally valued amid my value negations, I am freed from the harried need to defend myself; freed to hear the neighbor's claim. The self-deceptive rigidities under which guilt has carried on its clandestine operations are themselves disarmed by this freeing Word.

Christian consciousness experiences itself in a curious sense as *liberated to fail*, without intolerable damage to self-esteem and without any reduction of moral seriousness. We are free to be inadequate, free to foul things up, and yet affirm ourselves in a more basic sense than the secular moralist or humanistic idealist (who can affirm themselves only on the basis of merits and accomplishments). We are free to choose and deny finite values, free to take constructive guilt upon us and to see it as an inevitable and providentially given aspect of our fallen human condition.

All that we have said leads us to the pinnacle of this good news: *In Jesus Christ we need no longer be guilty before God. It is only before our clay-footed gods that we stand guilty!*

God has chosen to regard the whole fallen cosmos from the vantage point of its participation in Jesus Christ, according to Scripture (Rom. 5–8; Col. 1). However idolatrous we may be, our idolatry is only an attempted denial of who we are before God. We *are* persons whose value negations are judged and negated by the forgiving remembrance of God.

Two penetrating biblical analogies grasp the laughter of unmerited grace: It is as if humankind were standing before the Judge at the Endtime, deserving condemnation, but surprisingly the Judge himself is judged in our place! We are clothed in the Judge's own righteousness, as though enshrouded by that judicial cloak, regarded *as if* we were covered by that unimpeachable goodness!

Or, it is as if we were at a wedding. An unworthy bride (a harlot, according to the scriptural analogy) is being married to a fine, upstanding, respectable young bridegroom! The disreputable person (idolatrous humanity) receives as a wedding gift all the uprightness of the spouse (the messianic servant) *as if* it were her own. Likewise, before the source and end of values, our guilt is regarded *as if* it were absorbed and transformed by the righteousness of the bridegroom, Christ. The center of all classical theories of the atonement is: God himself takes our place, takes our guilt upon himself.

If this is so, what revised status does my past value negation now have? What reality does it possess before God, however rottenly I might happen to feel about it at the moment? It is wiped away, canceled out, X-ed off the ledger. One of the principal meanings of "forgiveness" in Greek is to X-out, or to cross off, a payment from the creditor's books.

The psychological experience of magnified guilt feelings is now perceived to be rooted in an absurdity, outmoded by the verdict of God's mercy. I may *feel* guilty before my gods, but I cannot *be* guilty before the forgiveness of God. Insofar as I continue to feel magnified guilt, I am living out an illusion.

Has the past been changed? Have value negations actually been wiped out or obliterated from history? Or are they merely "not counted" against the negator? Are they remembered *as if* they had not been done? Does the memory of God somehow mysteriously embrace the negated value, or is it lost forever?

In one sense, the past has not changed; only our perception of it has changed: For the past has always been objectively received into the forgiving memory of God. The Christ event did not in that sense *change* the will of God, but rather it more clearly expressed God's eternal will toward the whole of history. The New Testament reads history both forward and backward from the cross and resurrection of Christ. This is why the New Testament speaks of a "pre-existing" Word of God that exists before creation and time, but becomes revealed once for all in time. It is in response to this good news that we grasp what the past has always been for God from the beginning. Whereas we had been imagining that the past is composed of so many irreversible value losses that could only be mourned, now we see all things as embraced by the memory of God, so that "all things work together for good to them that love God" (Rom. 8:28*).

From this gift there follows a task: Whatever God allows to be received into his forgiving memory, I am called within the limits of my finitude to receive into my forgiving memory. Anything that God affirms, I am invited to affirm. Toward whatever God shows mercy, I am asked also to show mercy. This ethic is what took Albert Schweitzer to central Africa, Martin Luther King to the bus riders of Birmingham, and Mother Teresa to the poor of Calcutta.

The good news addresses the penitent sinner with a clear, divine Yes, not an ambiguous "blend of Yes and No." Jesus is "the Yes pronounced upon God's promises, every one of them" (II Cor. 1:19-20). The same merciful Lord is known in the Old Testament:

> The Lord is compassionate and gracious,
>   long-suffering and for ever constant;
>   he will not always be the accuser
>   or nurse his anger for all time.
> He has not treated us as our sins deserve
> or requited us for our misdeeds.
> For as the heaven stands high above the earth,
> so his strong love stands high over all who fear him.
>   Far as east is from west,
>   so far has he put our offences away from us.
>   (Ps. 103:8-12)

The distance from east to west was as far as the Hebraic mind could conceive of any distance being. That is how far our transgressions are removed

120

from us by God's love. They are "blotted out" (Ps. 51:1). "I . . . will remember your sins no more" (Isa. 43:25). All the transgressions that occasioned Israel's bondage were wiped out in God's mind, not remembered anymore. This experience formed the model of the historical memory out of which the New Testament understood Jesus' ministry as blotting out the sins of the whole world. Jesus was numbered among the transgressors (Isa. 53:12, quoted by Luke 22:37) that by his sacrificial action our transgressions might be forgiven and not remembered before God. God permitted his own son, Jesus, to be treated as a criminal and crucified in order that through his self-sacrificial suffering the sins of the whole world would be blotted out.

A similar image comes from Isaiah 44:22: "I have swept away your sins like a dissolving mist, and your transgressions are dispersed like clouds." What had once been a dangerous thunderstorm is now dispersed. What had once seemed to be the terror of guilt is now in God's sight blown away like clouds. "The former troubles are forgotten and they are hidden from my sight. For behold, I create new heavens and a new earth. Former things shall no more be remembered nor shall they be called to mind" (Isa. 65:16-17). This promise has been fulfilled, not only for the people of Israel, but for universal history in Jesus Christ. The implication is that if our trespasses are forgotten in God's eyes, we need not call them forever to mind.

Paul employs this powerful analogy: "You see, then, my brothers [and sisters] we are no slave-woman's children; our mother is the free woman.

121

Christ set us free, to be free [persons]. Stand firm, then, and refuse to be tied to the yoke of slavery again" (Gal. 4:31–5:1). Repeatedly Paul makes this point—in Romans, Corinthians, and throughout Galatians—that if we have been freed from guilt, we need no longer live *as if* we were guilty. "Where the Spirit of the Lord is, there is liberty" (II Cor. 3:17*). "The Lord laid upon him the guilt of us all" (Isa. 53:6). "The chastisement he bore is health for us and by his scourging we are healed" (v. 5).

"Happy the man whose disobedience is forgiven, whose sin is put away! Happy is a man when the Lord lays no guilt to his account, and in his spirit there is no deceit" (Ps. 32:1-2). Happiness comes from knowing that all the damage we have done to others and to ourselves is X-ed out. There is no loss column left in our account books. And there is no deceit about it, no attempt to pretend that we are better than we are. For God himself has taken on our guilt. This is why "the memory of the just is blessed" (Prov. 10:7*).

The Acquittal

Before whom am I guilty? Myself and my gods. But before God? I would be guilty before God *if* God had not disclosed himself as forgiving, taking my place, rendering a verdict of pardon upon me. But upon that *if* hinges the force of justification by grace through faith alone. For precisely amid our failure to actualize values we mistakenly imagine as ultimate, God himself continues to perceive us *as if* we were clothed in Christ's own righteousness. The Reformation formula, *simul peccator et justus,* meant:

I am a sinner, deserving condemnation for my idolatry; but from God's point of view I am *at the same time* pardoned, regarded as if the charge against me were canceled out! The final verdict is thus not the one I give myself or the one that may be given in the courts of law or gossip or peer pressure. Rather, it is what God himself has decided about my situation, how he has regarded and perceived me. Through God's own incomparable initiative, our sin is not remembered against us, even though we may oddly persist in remembering it against ourselves.

God's pardoning verdict is not merely an empty possibility which we may or may not actualize, but is already in the most literal sense an ever-present *actuality!* It is only on the premise that forgiveness is an actuality that it can truly become a possibility for us. In the Christ event the forgiving intent of God is made known once for all. Whether we hear the verdict or not, it is rendered. Whether we order our lives in terms of it or not, it is the proper center of all our life ordering.

Does this mean that the source and end of finite values simply condones everything in history, that there is no divine negation, that there exists in history a sentimental God who loves us despite all our stupidity and duplicity? That could be a dangerous invitation to irresponsibility.

No. God's resistance is directed against our gods, not ourselves, and more particularly it is against the willed idolatry by which certain good values have become misvalued. In the passionate metaphors of scripture, God "hates" our gods. He is a *jealous God.*

God gets *angry* when we go awhoring after sham gods. Note that God does not "hate" finite values as such—they are his own gift as Creator, good insofar as they are received as relative, finite, limited. The wrath of God is directed neither against creaturely values in themselves or persons as such but against our idolatrous self-assertive will through which we attempt to embody the stubborn illusion that we are not finite recipients of infinite love.

All talk about the wrath of God in the Bible intends to express the firm intention of God to challenge our idolatries, to show the vulnerability of these pretenses. Because God hates sin, he is determined to call us back into covenant. When we try repeatedly to affirm the impossible, to live absurdly as if we were not loved, the "anger" of God is directed against that illusion. For this reason, the pardon of God is never sentimental romanticism or lawless libertinism.

I am not arguing that there is no real guilt but merely guilt feelings. Rather, all of us are really guilty before our gods and live constantly amid the tragic, illusive, self-deceptive burden of that real guilt which causes us to withdraw from human intimacy for fear of being perceived as value bunglers.

But there is one thing that is not finally possible for us: to reduce to nothing the forgiveness of God, to flee the gracious covenant which circumscribes our existence, to relieve ourselves of the constraint of the friendly divine verdict. We cannot run away from that, because we cannot run away from ourselves. God continues to renew the covenant even when we break or neglect it. That is the story of

Hosea, of captive Israel and, symbolically, of all humanity.

The most we can do against the truth of God is to propound a lie. The most we can do against the concreteness of God's deed is to devise an *abstraction* by which we pretend that we are somehow abstracted out of the scene of the divine-human encounter that we call history.

The Scope of Pardon

The clearest statement of the wide scope of God's pardon is in the first letter of John: "Should anyone commit a sin, we have one to plead our cause with the Father, Jesus Christ, and he is just. He is himself the remedy for the defilement of our sins, not our sins only but the sins of all the world" (I John 2:1-2). God the Son advocates fallen humanity's cause before the Father. An advocate pleads the case of another. "Our sins only" means: We who have fellowship in him, who have heard the Word of life (I John 1:1), who proclaim eternal life (I John 1:2), who walk no longer in darkness (v. 5-7). The messianic judge and expiator is declared to be the guilt-bearer not for our sins only, but for the sins of the whole cosmos.

Summarizing the scope of God's reconciling action in his letter to Corinth, Paul writes: "All this is from God, who through Christ reconciled us to himself and gave us the ministry of reconciliation; that is, God was in Christ reconciling the world (*kosmos*) to himself, not counting their trespasses against them, and entrusting to us the message (*kerygma*) of reconciliation" (II Cor. 5:18-19

125

mar. h†). *Kosmos* means that whole order of creation which exists in enmity against God.

In the same passage Paul underscores the "all" (*pantos*) theme: "We are convinced that one has died for all; therefore all have died" (II Cor. 5:14†). He then integrates the divine gift (grace) and our human task (Jesus' claim on us) in this penetrating sentence: "And he died for all, that those who live might live no longer for themselves but for him who for their sake died and was raised" (v. 15).

Elsewhere Paul pushes the grace/claim question to its logical conclusion: "What if some were unfaithful? Does their faithlessness nullify the faithfulness of God? By no means! Let God be true though every [one] be false" (Rom. 3:3-4†). Is this cosmic scope of pardon an embarrassment to God, on the grounds that it lacks a rigorous sense of justice? Would not an unsurpassably just God find some more discriminating way of treating sin than unconditional mercy?

Nowhere is the inner consistency of mercy and grace more clearly stated than in Romans 3: "All . . . both Jews and Greeks, are under the power of sin" (Rom 3:9†). Yet it is only in the midst of the universal awareness of our value losses that "God's justice has been brought to light" (Rom. 3:21). Anticipated by both law and prophets, the gospel is

God's way of righting wrong, effective through faith in Christ for all who have such faith—all, without distinction. For all alike have sinned, and are deprived of the divine splendour, and all are justified by God's free grace alone, through his act of liberation in the person of Christ Jesus. For God designed him to be the means of expiating sin by his sacrificial death, effective through faith. God

126

meant by this to demonstrate his justice, because in his forebearance he had overlooked the sins of the past—to demonstrate his justice now in the present, showing that he is himself just and also justifies any man who puts his faith in Jesus. (Rom. 3:22-26)

The good news is not an artful dodge of justice, but an expression of a more fundamental justice refined to a higher degree. Rather than merely closing his eyes to our sin, God himself becomes attorney for us all. The act of pardon that is won in this advocacy intends to win our hearts in mercy toward others. "Freely have ye received, freely give" (Matt. 10:8*).

Our personal liberation, says Paul, is a preview of the liberty that the whole universe is ultimately destined to experience, even though now the created universe waits in expectation, in eager longing, for the final revelation of God. In the meantime the whole natural order has become infected by distortions of human freedom (note the demeaning effects upon nature of the misuse of our freedom in pollution, endangered species, the shrinking biosphere, the threat of nuclear annihilation, etc.). The whole universe has been adversely affected by the self-assertive abuses of human freedom. The whole universe, not merely our own personal sphere, will in due time share in the freedom from guilt that we now experience in Jesus Christ (Rom. 8:18-25). Similarly in Colossians: "Through him God chose to reconcile the whole universe to himself, making peace through the shedding of his blood upon the cross—to reconcile all things, whether on earth or in heaven, through him alone" (Col. 1:20).

This startling affirmation about Jesus has entered

127

deeply into the language of worship: "Behold the Lamb of God who taketh away the sins of the world" (John 1:29*). One sacrificial lamb is offered on behalf of all the people, and God receives this offering on behalf of all. Even though God's pardoning act is addressed to the whole world, however, it is possible for us still to "refuse to be comforted" (Ps. 77:2*). It is still possible for us to be "much cast down in [our] own eyes" (Neh. 6:16*). Indeed "the earth, O Lord, is full of thy mercy" (Ps. 119:64*), but that does not mean that we always understand it as such.

Does the gospel of forgiveness then tend toward a weak, sentimental, and overly optimistic idea of universal salvation in which God accepts all human lechery, avarice, pride, recalcitrance, evil, and insensitivity? No. Christian teaching makes a sharp distinction between *universal justification* and *actual salvation*: God's costly atoning work is declared and established for *all*, not some (Rom. 5; II Cor. 5:14ff.). It is unconditionally offered, whether or not we respond. And yet only *some* respond, answering it with their own will and behavior.

Salvation (from the Latin *salus*, health, wholeness) includes both justification and sanctification in that it involves not only the givenness of the divine verdict, but also the receptiveness of the human response to that verdict. Although doubtless it is intended for all, justification is not actually appropriated by all. Only some experientially participate in the wholeness of God, and reflect that wholeness in their behavior. But the Word is spoken for all to hear; the justifying deed is done for all. So Christian teaching is wary of an oversimple fantasy of *universal*

128

salvation, if salvation includes our actively willed participation in the saving deed of God. At the same time, there is scriptural warrant for *universal justification* (Col. 1; I John 2; Rom. 3, 5, 8; II Cor. 4–6), which remembers that the divine pardon is addressed to all. Not all receive what is given. But Christ died for all.

Meanwhile there is nothing in classical Christianity to prevent us from hoping that all might somehow be saved in some way that transcends our present vision.

If we insist on perceiving the dilemma of guilt strictly from our subjective and experiential side, then it is obvious that there are tremendous human resources which are continually wasted, never to be situationally recovered. Abstracted from the divine pardoning verdict, the human past remains unalterably fixed in wretched bondage to value negation. The only reasonable attitude to adopt toward it is despair.

But if we perceive the same guilt more broadly from the perspective of God's atoning action, our past is an entirely different matter. The deeper ground of human experiencing from which the guilt-burdened individual can never succeed in escaping is this: the mercy of God who loves us amid our gravest moral irresponsibilities in a way that calls us to wider moral responsibilities.

Where Does Liberty End and License Begin?

The gospel offers us the freedom to reject beneficial values, to freely ignore some legitimate responsibilities in favor of others, to deny relative goods in order that better situational goods might be achieved. Within careful limits, this is what the New Testament authorizes with its ringing affirmation that Christ is the end of the law, in the sense of the end of self-destructive attitudes toward exalted duties and idealized requirements which prevent us from loving the neighbor "as is." Seeking carefully to avoid abusing its own freedom, the Christian life joyfully affirms a guilt-free *capacity to deny* certain goods in order to receive or create other goods, in an ever-new responsiveness to unfolding reality.

This is why Christian freedom can celebrate situational losses of value as well as modest value achievements. The student whose responsible political activities have cost him crucial study time may take a failure on a quiz without a disastrous scar to his whole self-esteem, freely affirming the failure as consistent with a broader self-understanding which regards neither the political process nor the academic mark as a final value by which other values are ultimately to be judged. The compulsively productive businessman whose only joy has been the creation of wealth now finds himself freed under the forgiving Word to value himself in spite of his lapses into unproductivity.

But . . . are we thus opening the door to lying, thievery, self-assertion, sexual license, and a Pandora's box of moral junk under the benign guise of divine forgiveness? Shall we sin that grace may abound (not a new question for Christian liberty)? To return to the pressing social concerns of chapter 1: How can we establish safeguards against the trampling of hard-won, richly hewn, social values and moral traditions without exalting them to absolutes? Genuine Christian freedom recognizes the need for such careful safeguards and, in fact, fights hard to protect them. When Christian freedom is turned into laxity or license in the name of unconditional love, it tends to self-destruct. It becomes undisciplined, careless, spurious freedom. The scrupulous distinction between Christian freedom and *antinomian* (irresponsible, lawless, anarchic) pseudofreedom has been wrestled with for many generations of scriptural interpreters from Augustine's *The Spirit and the Letter* through Luther's *Treatise on Good Works* to Kierkegaard's *Works of Love*. Minimally it must be said that genuine evangelical freedom exists amid covenant cohumanity with the neighbor, and always with grateful protection of the social and legal structures through which the neighbor's interests are guarded. If the word of forgiveness becomes a low-cost invitation to anarchic irresponsibility so as to ignore the neighbor's safety and welfare, then we have failed to hear the ethical notes in the rich chord of divine pardon.

The good news presents us a personal invitation to profound self-affirmation (deeper than humanistic). At face value, this may seem to stand opposed to the respected ascetic tradition in Christian history which has stressed *self-denial*. There remains a rich store of wisdom in the Monastic and Puritan traditions of self-denial which we ignore to our peril, especially in a crunch economy that will ask us to do more with less. We have much to learn from ascetic masters about the reduction of desire and the happiness of thinking small. But self-denial is not itself the final goal of the Christian life; rather, it is a preparation for faith and a response to faith. No believer was ever saved by self-denial. But neither does anyone become a mature Chrisian without it (Matt. 16:24; Mark 8:34). The traditions of self-affirmation and self-denial are richly complementary. The most accountable and self-giving relation to the neighbor occurs on the basis of a profound self-affirmation rooted in God's own affirmation of the self, which is on that basis capable of acts of sacrifice and self-emptying agape.

Any talk of guilt-free liberation must be fine-tuned by the scriptural claim that we are to "live as free [persons]; not however as though your freedom were there to provide a screen for wrongdoing, but as slaves in God's service" (I Peter 2:16). We are called to exercise Christian freedom energetically, as we would exercise a muscle, but not to allow it to become a subterfuge by which we assert our own interests under the guise of divine pardon.

Wherever the early church proclaimed the guilt-free promise of life in Christ, it has always had to couple it with a plain warning against the abuses of freedom. Nowhere in the Bible is Christian freedom more commended than in Galatians. But precisely there Paul warns: "You, my friends, were called to be free men [and women]; only do not turn your freedom into licence for your lower nature, but be servants to one another in love. For the whole law can be summed up in a single commandment: 'Love your neighbor as yourself' " (Gal. 5:13-14). Pauline psychology was keenly aware that the sinful will, the part of us that "naturally" wants to assert our interest first, is prone to take even the liberty of forgiveness and make of it an "occasion of the flesh." He implored the Corinthians to:

132

Be careful that this liberty of yours does not become a
pitfall for the weak. If a weak character sees you sitting
down to a meal in a heathen temple—you, who "have
knowledge"—will not his conscience be emboldened to
eat food consecrated to the heathen deity? This "knowledge" of yours is utter disaster to the weak, the brother
[and sister] for whom Christ died. In thus sinning against
your brothers [and sisters] and wounding their conscience, you sin against Christ. (I Cor. 8:10-12)

When we flaunt our liberation from guilt in such a
way as to injure the conscience of those who have
not fully entered into Christian freedom, we can do
grave damage quickly.

Paul identified most of the main shortcuts by
which Christian freedom could be (and still is being)
abused. While not letting up on his stress on "the
glorious liberty of the children of God," Paul makes
this astonishing distinction: "I am free to do
anything. . . . Yes, but not everything is for my
good. No doubt I am free to do anything, but I for
one will not let anything make free with me" (I Cor.
6:12). Elsewhere translated: " 'All things are lawful
for me,' but I will not be enslaved by anything."† "I
may do everything, but I must not be a slave of
anything" (Phillips). What does this mean? Nothing
is beyond the range of God's pardon; but that does
not mean that anything I might do would be good
for me or others, or an appropriate expression of
the freedom to love. Genuine freedom is not merely
doing what I want but what I *ought*.

"Shall we persist in sin, so that there may be all the
more grace?" Why not, if God pardons all? Why not
take advantage, and "live it up?" No, no, protests
Paul. "We died to sin: how can we live in it any
longer?" (Rom. 6:1-2). Paul's answer hinges on this

unusual analogy: It is as if in baptism you have died to the old aeon, the old way of life, and are living in a new age in which God's pardoning gift has been given. Why then live as if the new age had not begun? (Rom. 6:3-11).

In the same letter Paul refines a delicate point: The problem is not with the law itself, but with sin willfully existing in a distorted relation to the law. "The law is in itself holy, and the commandment is holy and just and good" (Rom. 7:12). So do not target God's law as an object of blame for your sinfulness. "We know that the law is spiritual; but I am not" (Rom. 7:14).

The preaching of forgiveness can become an immoral disaster if unaccompanied by an earnest effort to nurture a community of forgiving love in which God's mercy is enacted in Word, Sacrament, and caring relationships. This reawakens the useful old distinction between justification and sanctification, i.e., between what God does *for* us, and what God does *in* us; between God's atoning, justifying act of pardon in Jesus Christ, and the work of the Holy Spirit in calling us to responsiveness to that work in our own deeds, so that faith in Christ's work produces in us the fruits of love (see Luther's *Christian Liberty* and Calvin's *Institutes*, Books II and III).

The New Birth of Memory

It is only when the past is itself regarded as reconstituted that a genuinely new memory is possible. The pardoning verdict of God does precisely that. It frees the human memory to view the past and all its tragic value negations as embraced by the pardon and grace of God. When we accept this gift, we can embrace our own value negations as having been embraced by God.

If physical birth is the beginning of memory and indeed an event in which all things are made new, then we can say that the reception of forgiveness is very much like a new birth of memory. The renewed memory is now freed to explore the entire range of the personal and cosmic past, to receive it without demoralization or fear, in the confidence that it is taken up in its totality into the gracious will of God. The new birth of memory under the address of divine forgiveness, therefore, is an ever-recurring birth, a natal openness to every emerging now. To imagine ourselves without a past is to imagine being born again.

Human memory exists in the context of the memory of God. Aware or unaware, all our remembering is a fragmented, broken, partial dimension of the perfect and total cosmic remembering of God. What remains as a negation of value in our past is received affirmatively into the memory of God. Thus the profoundest dimension of human memory is to be understood under the analogy of faith: the incompleteness of our remembering exists within the completeness of God's own pardoning memory of the cosmic totality.

☆ ☆ ☆ ☆ ☆

The heart of the difference between cheap-grace doctrines of guilt-free existence and the Christian gospel is this: Modern chauvinism desperately avoids the message of guilt by treating it as a regrettable symptom. Christianity intently listens to the message of guilt by conscientious self-examination. Hedonism winks at sin. Christianity earnestly confesses sin. Secularism assumes it can extricate itself from gross misdeeds. Christianity looks to grace for divine forgiveness. Modern consciousness is its own fumbling attorney before the bar of conscience. Christianity rejoices that God himself has become our attorney. Modernity sees no reason to atone for or make reparation for wrongs. Christianity knows that unatoned sin brings on misery of conscience. Modern naturalism sees no need for God. Christianity celebrates God's willingness to suffer for our sins and redeem us from guilt.

Epilogue

The Peril of Unreceived Pardon
A Parable

Jesus' Parable of the Unmerciful Servant (Matt. 18:21-35†) has the unique advantage of taking seriously the very point which has thus far been the most hazardous trap of all guilt-free rhetoric: the pivotal importance of receiving personal pardon in a way that does not neglect social responsibility.

Let us imagine that we are viewing three brief scenes of a motion picture that moves very rapidly and yet shows a clear dramatic development through ten frames of concise action.

Scene One: A Servant Pleads for Patience

Frame One: The prologue: The subject under discussion is the final day of history, which is compared to a king who has decided to settle his accounts. The setting: The end of time. Anyone who owes anything is now required to pay.

137

Frame Two: The scene quickly focuses on a certain servant who owes his lord a fantastic sum (ten thousand talents would be one hundred million denarii, perhaps ten million dollars), a debt almost impossible to calculate and totally beyond the range of the poor debtor's resources. This reminds us of the immensity of our own indebtedness as value negators.

Frame Three: In an instant, the lord orders him to be sold as a slave, with his family and all his possessions, in order that something of value might be salvaged from the bad debt. Like a banker's cool examination of the value of a man's possessions in order to know whether he can lend him money, the question suddenly becomes "What are you worth?" The average value of a slave was from five hundred to two thousand denarii. He owes one hundred million denarii. Well, obviously everything he has and is cannot begin to pay his account. The end-time settlement requires that we pay up what we do not have, so we are being asked to pay with our very selves. Our indebtedness brings suffering and slavery not only to us but to our loved ones as well. It is to such a final reckoning that we are being summoned.

Frame Four: The servant falls prostrate at his master's feet and implores: "Be patient with me, and I will pay in full." He is asking for time in order to make up the losses—time to perform the required duty (not for forgiveness—that never occurred to him). How our sympathies are drawn to this pitiable figure! He fears the harsh judgment in which he is already caught. However inadequate his resources, he promises to pay in full. But it is the endtime.

There is no time for patience or more hard work. The account must be settled.

Frame Five: Moved to pity by the servant's plea, the lord cancels the debt and sets the poor man and his family free. With dramatic swiftness, in one bold single stroke, the lord changes the whole objective situation of the debt. He renders an unexpected verdict: pardon. The debt is suddenly wiped off the books! In an instant the poor servant is unburdened of all the penalties the vast debt had incurred.

Mark carefully: If a debt is canceled, then it is impossible for one to be indebted! It is the creditor who controls the debt. Likewise, if the giver of values pardons our wretched value losses, then there is nothing that we can do to be guilty. We may (absurdly) continue to feel indebted, even though the debt is canceled, but as a matter of fact there is no further debt, since the debt is not finally in the hands of the debtor but the creditor. Any subjective feelings of continued indebtedness are simply groundless. So ends the first scene, but the action is only beginning.

Scene Two: The Forgiven Servant Meets a Fellow-Debtor

Frame Six: As the servant walks away, it is presumably the hope of the lord that his mercy and forgiveness will elicit a like attitude of mercy and forgiveness in the servant. But the central surprise of the parable now appears, and the premise of the whole story becomes curiously inverted. "No sooner had the man gone out than he met a fellow-servant who owed him a few pounds; and catching hold of him he gripped him by the throat and said, 'Pay me what you owe.' "

No sooner had the man gone out! One would guess that he would be so grateful to receive his life back again that he would gladly give away all that he had, and quickly cancel the petty debts that others owed him. His problem was that he never really understood what had happened to him, never fully comprehended that he was a free and pardoned man! He did not respond to the actual, forgiving reality at hand. Rather he chose to live in his own abstract and absurd world of petty legalism.

Seizing the fellow-debtor by the throat he said, "Pay what you owe." Jesus sharpens the contrast. What does the fellow-servant owe? One hundred denarii (Phillips: "a few shillings")! He himself had owed one hundred million denarii but a few moments ago—more than the total value of all his possessions and his family sold in slavery! Let us not miss the irony of this absurd comparison. He is now demanding a paltry debt of one-millionth the value of his own indebtedness. So little does he understand the depth of what has just happened to him that he cannot hear the simpler need of his neighbor.

Frame Seven: The fellow-servant falls prostrate at his feet and implores him: "Be patient with me, and I will pay you." That sounds familiar. In fact, it is precisely the same plea which he himself made a moment ago. Surely he will hear this virtual echo of his own voice. The comparison is strictly drawn: he is being called to offer to others the same forgiveness that was offered to him. From here, events follow swiftly.

140

Frame Eight: The servant refused and went and put him in prison till he should pay the debt. Harshly he cuts off even the possibility of paying the debt. He does not even offer to explore any other alternatives. His merciless obstinacy contrasts with the openness and mercy of the king. His brutal, imprisoning action is just as abrupt as the king's liberating decision. With a wave of a hand the fellow-servant is now in a dungeon, just as with the wave of the lord's hand the servant was a moment ago instantly freed.

Patience is a virtue that exists in time, that willingly allows time to pass while awaiting expected value actualizations. But the servant has no time, no patience. Like the king, he wants to settle his accounts. The endtime is at hand. The kingdom of God is a time like this. It calls for a radical decision for the neighbor.

Scene Three: The Final Reckoning

Frame Nine: When his fellow-servants saw what had taken place, they were greatly distressed, and they went and reported to their lord all that had taken place. They did not go to accuse, but merely to report. They were distressed that such a great gift was so poorly received that the spirit of the gift could not be shared even in the slightest way with the fellow-servant.

The lord summoned the man and said: "You wicked servant! I forgave you all that debt because you besought me; and should not you have had mercy on your fellow-servant, as I had mercy on you?" Haven't you misunderstood the situation out of which you have just been extricated? Shouldn't

141

you care for others in the same way that you have been cared for?

Frame Ten: The lord hands over the man to the torturers, until the debt is paid. The torturers are the demonic powers. This is a symbolic way of saying that when genuine love cannot make its presence known in the life of a person, when he blocks himself off from the offer of forgiveness, then he finds himself by his own decision handed over to the destructive power of despairing guilt. The judge then judges the first debtor by the same standard the first has applied to the second debtor, as if to say, "If you have not learned to respond to mercy, then have a taste of your own medicine. Maybe you will learn through the pain of despairing guilt how important it is to pass along to others the mercy you have received."

This does not mean that the pardoning verdict is rescinded. It means rather that it has never been accepted, that its recipient has chosen to live under his previous circumstances of indebtedness. The man merely confirms the legalistic self-understanding he has had from the beginning. Until the servant pays his debt in some fashion (either under his own legalistic terms or in receipt of the Lord's pardon), he will continue to be tormented. But he himself has insisted upon the mode by which the account is to be paid. The parable shows that the insensitive servant is determined to be judged by his own petty legalistic criteria instead of the freedom-bestowing spirit of forgiveness.

Far from arguing that the forgiveness of God is conditional upon our reception of it, the parable suggests that anyone who truly hears the word of forgiveness will be found sharing it joyfully with his neighbor. If he does not, he simply excludes himself from its benefits and condemns himself to the burden of guilt.

Unmistakably this is a parable of the relation of grace and responsibility, of gospel and law. Here is a man who thinks he exists strictly under the law. When he pleads for time, it is only a plea for time to fulfill the law. He is indeed guilty under the law, and if that is as far as he can see, obviously he needs more time. But the truth is, he has no time. It is the endtime, the time for a final settling of accounts. Normal rules of business do not apply. He grossly misunderstands the situation in which he actually exists. He is being called to pardon as he is pardoned. But all this is impossible for him to fit into his harshly legalistic self-understanding. So the moment he is met by a fellow-debtor who calls him to forgive as he has been forgiven, his mind jumps to the old legalisms. So he tragically places the same law upon his neighbor under which he has mistakenly understood himself to be placed, and this is his damnation. The king in effect says, "So be it—let him live under the law if he must, let him be judged by his own damning criteria for righteousness, by his own deeds! He has his reward!" He has thereby chosen not to enter into the new age of the governance of God.

We return to the central question which motivated Jesus to tell the parable: "Peter approached him with the question, 'Master, how many times can my brother wrong me and I must forgive him? Would seven times be enough?' 'No,' replied Jesus, 'not seven times, but seventy times seven! For the kingdom of Heaven is like a king who decided to settle his accounts with his servants' " (Matt. 18:21-23, Phillips).

The final frame of the drama makes one simple, piercing point: "This is how my heavenly Father will treat you unless you each forgive your brother [and sister] from your heart." And indeed it is so. If we fail to respond to the reality of forgiveness, this is what happens to us. If we insist upon living under the guilt-laden grip of legalism and idolatry, we pay the price.

So as it often happens, Jesus, by telling a simple story, keeps all the complex factors of the discussion of guilt and freedom in perfect balance. Guilt is embraced by grace, yet grace summons us to comfort others as we have been comforted.